The wolf shall dwell with the lamb,
and the leopard shall lie down with the kid,
and the calf and the lion and the fatling together,
and a little child shall lead them.

Isaiah 11:6

THE MEANING of the MILLENNIUM:

FOUR VIEWS

EDITED BY ROBERT G. CLOUSE

with
contributions
by
George Eldon Ladd
Herman A. Hoyt
Loraine Boettner
Anthony A. Hoekema

InterVarsity Press
Downers Grove
Illinois 60515

InterVarsity Press is the book-publishing division of Inter-Varsity Christian Fellowship, a student movement active on campus at hundreds of universities, colleges and schools of nursing. For information about local and regional activities, write IVCF, 233 Langdon St., Madison, WI 53703.

Distributed in Canada through InterVarsity Press, 1875 Leslie St., Unit 10, Don Mills, Ontario M3B 2M5, Canada.

Biblical quotations are from the Revised Standard Version of the Bible, copyrighted 1946, 1952, © 1971, 1973 by the Division of Christian Education, National Council of the Churches of Christ in the U.S.A.

ISBN 0-87784-794-0
Library of Congress Catalog Card Number: 76-55556

Printed in the United States of America

20   19   18   17   16   15   14   13
94   93   92   91   90   89

INTRODUCTION
ROBERT G. CLOUSE

One of the more difficult themes with which interpreters of the Bible must deal is the teaching of the kingdom of God. The problem is brought into sharp focus when the believer gives his or her explanation of such passages as Daniel 2 and Revelation 20. Attempts to relate these texts to the course of human history have led Christians to fashion a number of different systems explaining the return of Christ and his reign, three of which have been labeled premillennial, amillennial and postmillennial. These categories, although helpful and widely accepted, are in certain respects unfortunate as the distinctions involve a great deal more than the time of Christ's return. The kingdom expected by the premillennialist is quite different from the kingdom anticipated by the postmillennialist, not only with respect to the time and manner in which it will be established but also in regard to its nature and the way Christ will exercise control over it. These views and their implications can be understood more clearly by defining them in detail.

Some Brief Definitions
Premillennialists generally believe that the return of Christ will be preceded by certain signs such as the preaching of the

gospel to all nations, a great apostasy, wars, famines, earth-quakes, the appearance of the Antichrist and a great tribula-tion. His return will be followed by a period of peace and righteousness before the end of the world. Christ will reign as King in person or through a select group of followers. This reign, rather than being established by the conversion of indi-vidual souls over a long period of time, will come about sud-denly and by overwhelming power. The Jews will be convert-ed and will become very important during this time. Nature will also share in the millennial blessings by being abundantly productive. Even ferocious beasts will be tamed. Evil is held in check during this age by Christ who rules with "a rod of iron." However, at the end of the millennium there is a rebellion of wicked men which almost overwhelms the saints. Some pre-millennialists have taught that during this golden age dead believers will be resurrected with their glorified bodies to mingle freely with the rest of the inhabitants of the earth. After the millennium the non-Christian dead are raised and the eternal states of heaven and hell are established.

In contrast to the premillennialist, the postmillennialist explains that the kingdom of God is now being extended through Christian teaching and preaching. This activity will cause the world to be Christianized and result in a long period of peace and prosperity called the millennium. The new age will not be essentially different from the present. It emerges as an increasing proportion of the world's inhabitants are con-verted to Christianity. Evil is not eliminated but will be re-duced to a minimum as the moral and spiritual influence of Christians is heightened. The church will assume greater im-portance and many social, economic and educational prob-lems will be solved. This period closes with the Second Com-ing of Christ, the resurrection of the dead and the final judgment.

Amillennialists hold that the Bible does not predict a period of universal peace and righteousness before the end of the world. They believe that there will be a continuous growth of good and evil in the world which will culminate in the Second Coming of Christ when the dead shall be raised and the last judgment held. Amillennialists hold that the kingdom of God is now present in the world as the victorious Christ is ruling his people by his Word and Spirit, though they also look forward to a future, glorious and perfect kingdom on the new earth in the life to come. Amillennialists interpret the millennium mentioned in Revelation 20 as describing the present reign of the souls of deceased believers with Christ in heaven.

Different Views at Different Times
Although these interpretations have never been without adherents in the history of the church, in certain ages a particular outlook has predominated. During the first three centuries of the Christian era, premillennialism appears to have been the dominant eschatological interpretation. Among its adherents were Papias, Irenaeus, Justin Martyr, Tertullian, Hippolytus, Methodius, Commodianus and Lactantius. During the fourth century when the Christian church was given a favored status under the emperor Constantine, the amillennial position was accepted. The millennium was reinterpreted to refer to the church, and the thousand-year reign of Christ and his saints was equated with the whole history of the church on earth, thus making for the denial of a future millennium. The famous church father, Augustine, articulated this position, and it became the dominant interpretation in medieval times. His teaching was so fully accepted that at the Council of Ephesus in 431, belief in the millennium was condemned as superstitious.

Even though official Church doctrine was amillennial, during the Middle Ages premillennialism continued among certain groups of believers. At times these millennialists used their teaching to strike at the establishment. For example, in areas whose population increased as traditional social bonds were shattered by differences in wealth, the desire for the millennium of peace and security became intense. Under leaders who claimed to be inspired by the Holy Spirit, the anxiety caused by new social conditions resulted in attempts to rebel against the oppressors in the name of God and in pursuit of the millennium.[1] One of the last examples of this activity was a rebellion in the city of Münster in 1534. A man named Jan Matthys took control of the community preaching that he was Enoch preparing the way for the return of Christ by establishing a community of good and doing away with the prevailing law codes. Then he issued a call for all the faithful to gather at Münster because it was the New Jerusalem. A great multitude of Anabaptists fled to the city and were besieged by an army of both Protestants and Catholics. A reign of terror served to keep the community under the control of Matthys's successor, Jan Bockelson, but the defenses finally collapsed and the town was taken.

Perhaps this episode led the Protestant Reformers to stay with Augustinian amillennialism. However, they did inaugurate changes in eschatological interpretation which set the stage for a great renewal of premillennial interest during the seventeenth century. Martin Luther (1483-1546), for example, advocated a more literal approach to the Scriptures, identified the papacy with the Antichrist and called attention to Bible prophecies. Some later Lutheran scholars redirected this interest to focus on a premillennial interpretation. John Calvin (1509-1564), like Luther, was very cautious in his approach to millenarian interpretations, possibly because of the excesses of some of the Anabaptists.[2]

Despite his opposition, it was a German Calvinist theologian, Johann Heinrich Alsted (1588-1638), who revived the teaching of premillennialism in an academic form in the

modern world.[3] Alsted's book, *The Beloved City* (1627), which
presented his views, caused the learned Anglican scholar, Joseph Mede (1586-1638), to become a premillennialist. The
works of both men helped to inspire the desire for God's kingdom on earth which accompanied the outbreak of the Puritan
Revolution of the 1640s.[4] However, with the restoration of the
Stuart rulers, this outlook was discredited due to its connection with radical Puritan groups such as the Fifth Monarchy
Men. Even so, premillennialism was not extinct in the eighteenth century as evidenced by the interest of J. H. Bengel,
Isaac Newton and Joseph Priestley.

As premillennialism waned, postmillennialism became the
prevailing eschatological interpretation receiving its most impressive formulation through the work of Daniel Whitby
(1638-1726). According to his interpretation, the world was
to be converted to Christ, the Jews restored to their land, and
the pope and Turks defeated, after which the earth would
enjoy a time of universal peace, happiness and righteousness
for a thousand years. At the close of this period Christ would
return personally for the last judgment. Perhaps because of
its agreement with the views of the eighteenth-century En-
lightenment, postmillennialism was adopted by the leading
commentators and preachers of the age.[5]

During the nineteenth century premillennialism again at-
tracted widespread attention. This interest was fostered by
the violent uprooting of European political and social institutions during the era of the French Revolution.[6] There was also
a renewed interest in the conversion and status of the Jews.
One of the more influential leaders at this time was Edward
Irving (1792-1834), a Church of Scotland minister who served
a church in London, published many works on prophecy and
helped to organize the Albury Park prophecy conferences.
These meetings set the pattern for millennial gatherings
throughout the nineteenth and twentieth centuries. The pro-

phetic enthusiasm of Irving spread to other groups and found firm support among the Plymouth Brethren movement.

J. N. Darby (1800-1882), an early Plymouth Brethren leader, articulated the dispensationalist understanding of premillennialism. He described the coming of Christ before the millennium as consisting of two stages: the first, a secret rapture removing the church before the Great Tribulation devastates the earth; the second, Christ's coming with his saints to set up the kingdom. He also believed that the church is a mystery of which only Paul spoke and that the purposes of God in Scripture could be understood through a series of time periods called dispensations. At his death Darby left forty volumes of writings and some fifteen hundred assemblies around the world. Through his books, which include four volumes on prophecy, the dispensational system was carried throughout the English-speaking world. The line of continuity from Darby to the present can be traced from his dispensationalist contemporaries and followers (C. H. Mackintosh, William Kelly and F. W. Grant) through the interceding scholars (W. E. Blackstone, James Hall Brooks, G. Campbell Morgan, H. A. Ironside, A. C. Gaebelein, and C. I. Scofield and his Scofield Bible) to the current adherents of his views.[7] The extent of this influence has been so vast that in many evangelical circles today the dispensationalist interpretation prevails. The spread of Darby's views was aided by Henry Moorhouse, a Brethren evangelist of dispensational outlook, who helped convince D. L. Moody (1837-1899) of his prophetic interpretation. By the end of the nineteenth century Moody was probably the outstanding leader among evangelicals. Darby's impact on C. I. Scofield (1843-1921) was probably even more important since Scofield made dispensationalism an integral part of his Bible notes, and within fifty years three million copies of the *Scofield Reference Bible* were printed in the United States.[8] In recent days the popularity of

Hal Lindsey's books again demonstrates the vitality of the dispensational view.[9]

Each of the systems which have been briefly mentioned in historic context has had devout evangelical Christian adherents. The situation remains the same today. The following essays are offered as statements of each position by staunch believers who also hold to the millennial views they express. Professor George Eldon Ladd of Fuller Theological Seminary presents what could be called "historic" premillennialism. Chancellor Herman A. Hoyt of Grace Theological Seminary writes about "dispensational" premillennialism. Loraine Boettner discusses the postmillennial view. A final essay by Professor Anthony A. Hoekema of Calvin Theological Seminary elaborates the amillennial position. At the conclusion of each of the articles the other contributors respond from their particular viewpoints. In addition, after a final word from myself, there is a selected bibliography of millennialist literature.

It is my hope that these articles will aid the serious student of Scripture in formulating his or her own conclusions concerning the interpretation of the millennium. The exposition of prophecy is an area of Christian doctrine in which the warning of Paul must always be kept in mind: "For now we see in a mirror dimly, but then face to face. Now I know in part; then I shall understand fully, even as I have been fully understood" (1 Cor. 13:12).

I
HISTORIC PREMILLENNIALISM

HISTORIC PREMILLENNIALISM
GEORGE ELDON LADD

Premillennialism is the doctrine stating that after the Second Coming of Christ, he will reign for a thousand years over the earth before the final consummation of God's redemptive purpose in the new heavens and the new earth of the Age to Come. This is the natural reading of Revelation 20:1-6.

Revelation 19:11-16 pictures the Second Coming of Christ as a conqueror coming to destroy his enemies: the Antichrist, Satan and Death. Revelation 19:17-21 pictures first the destruction of Antichrist and the hosts which have supported him in opposition to the kingdom of God. Revelation 20 then relates the destruction of the evil power behind the Antichrist —"the dragon, that ancient serpent, who is the Devil and Satan" (Rev. 20:2). This occurs in two stages.

First, Satan is bound and incarcerated in "the bottomless pit" (Rev. 20:1) for a thousand years "that he should deceive the nations no more" (Rev. 20:3) as he had done through Antichrist. At this time occurs the "first resurrection" (Rev. 20:5) of saints who share Christ's rule over the earth for the thousand years. After this Satan is loosed from his bonds, and in spite of the fact that Christ has reigned over the earth for a thousand years, he finds the hearts of unregenerated men still ready to rebel against God. The final eschatological war follows when the devil is thrown into the lake of fire and brimstone. Then occurs a second resurrection of those who had not been raised before the millennium. They appear before the judgment throne of God to be judged according to their works. "If any one's name was not found written in the book of life, he was thrown into the lake of fire" (Rev. 20:15). Then Death and the grave were thrown into the lake of fire.

Thus Christ wins his victory over his three enemies: Antichrist, Satan and Death. Only then, when all hostile powers have been subdued, is the scene ready for the eternal state—the coming of the new heaven and new earth (Rev. 21:1-4). This is the most natural reading of Revelation 20, and most "preterist" interpreters (those who understand the book to be a typical Jewish-Christian, first-century apocalypse and not a Christian prophecy of the end times) generally understand it in this way.

For those who regard it as a Christian prophecy of the actual consummation of God's redemptive purpose, a further question remains. What other Scriptures teach a millennial reign of Christ? What other Scriptures can we draw on to find out what will be the nature of this reign?

The Question of Hermeneutics
In answer to these questions there is among evangelical scholars a sharp difference of opinion, and there are thus very different answers given. Dispensational theory insists that many of the Old Testament prophecies predict the millennium and must be drawn in to construct the picture of Messiah's millennial reign. This view is based upon the hermeneutic that the Old Testament prophecies must be interpreted literally. Charles Ryrie, one of the more articulate spokesmen

for dispensational theology, has made this very clear in his book, *Dispensationalism Today.*[1]

The first *sine qua non* of dispensationalism is the distinction between Israel and the church. Ryrie agrees with Daniel Fuller who says that "the basic premise of Dispensationalism is two purposes of God expressed in the formation of two peoples who maintain their distinction throughout eternity."[2] This conclusion rests upon a second principle: that of a literal system of biblical interpretation.[3] This, however, has primary application to the Old Testament. The Old Testament promises that Israel will be God's people forever, that they will inherit the land of Palestine forever, that they will form God's theocratic kingdom forever. These predictions will be fulfilled in the millennium.

The opposite to a literal hermeneutic of the Old Testament is a "spiritualizing" hermeneutic, that is, a hermeneutic which finds the Old Testament prophecies fulfilled in the Christian church. Thus amillennialists usually find a "spiritual" interpretation of the millennium. The millennium is not a literal reign of Christ on the earth; it is either the reign of Christ in this age in his church, or it is the reign of the martyrs after death in the intermediate state.

The seriousness of this problem for the dispensationalist is seen in a quotation from Walvoord:

The modernist who spiritualizes the resurrection of Christ does so by almost the same techniques as are used by B. B. Warfield who finds heaven described in Revelation 20: 1-10. Further, the history of modern liberalism has demonstrated that its adherents are drawn almost entirely from amillennial ranks.[4]

Walvoord goes on to say that "the diverse theological systems of Roman Catholic, modern liberal, and modern conservative writers are found to be using essentially the same method."[5] This amounts to the claim that only dispensationalism, with its literal hermeneutic of the Old Testament, can provide a truly evangelical theology.

In my view this simply is not true. B. B. Warfield did not use the same "spiritualizing" hermeneutic as the liberal. The liberal *admits* that the New Testament teaches the bodily resurrection of Christ, but his philosophical presuppositions make it impossible for him to accept it. On the other hand, B. B. Warfield was the greatest exponent of a high view of biblical inspiration of his day. He was prepared to accept any doctrine which could be proved by the Scriptures. If he "spiritualized" the millennium, it was because he felt *a total biblical hermeneutic required him to do so.* This is not liberalism. It is a question where equally evangelical scholars who accept the Bible as the inspired Word of God should be able to disagree without the accusation "liberal."

Ryrie correctly identified myself as a nondispensationalist because I do not keep Israel and the church distinct throughout God's program; but I trust that my evangelical stance is not thereby suspect.[6] In the study of the millennium I am prepared to accept whatever anyone can establish as biblical teaching; and if I do not accept dispensational distinctives, it is because I feel compelled by the inspired Word of God not to do so. Let this be clear: the Bible and the Bible alone is our one authority.

One of the chief arguments for interpreting the Old Testament prophecies concerning the end is that the Old Testament prophecies about the first coming of Christ were literally fulfilled. This, however, is an argument which must be closely examined. The fact is that the New Testament frequently interprets Old Testament prophecies in a way *not suggested by the Old Testament context.*

Let us take first a very simple illustration. Matthew 2:15 quotes from Hosea 11:1 to prove from Scripture that Jesus must come from Egypt. This, however, is not what the prophecy means in the Old Testament. Hosea says, "When Israel was a child, I loved him, and out of Egypt I called my son." In Hosea this is not a prophecy at all but a historical affirmation that God had called Israel out of Egypt in the Exodus. However, Matthew recognizes Jesus to be God's greater son and deliberately turns a historical statement into a prophecy. This is a principle which runs throughout biblical prophecy. *The Old Testament is reinterpreted* in light of the Christ event.

Let us look at a more significant illustration. The New Testament and the Christian church see a prophecy of the sufferings of the Messiah in Isaiah 53. Matthew applies this prophecy to Jesus (Mt. 8:17) although he does not refer to the sufferings to be endured by the servant. However, Philip interprets the sufferings of the servant to the Ethiopian eunuch as referring to Jesus (Acts 8:30-35).

How can anyone avoid recognizing that Isaiah 53 is a prophecy of the sufferings Jesus experienced?

But he was wounded for our transgressions,
    he was bruised for our iniquities;
upon him was the chastisement that made us whole,
    and with his stripes we are healed.
All we like sheep have gone astray;
    We have turned everyone to his own way;
and the Lord has laid on him
    the iniquity of us all. (Is. 53:5-6)

It is of course true that this is a prophecy of Jesus' sufferings but only as it is interpreted after the event. Here is another illustration of the New Testament interpreting the Old Testament in light of the Christ event. The simple fact is, in its Old Testament setting, Isaiah 53 is not a prophecy of the Messiah. *Messiah* means "anointed" and designates the victorious, anointed Davidic king. This is seen clearly in Isaiah 11.

He shall not judge by what his eyes see,
    or decide by what his ears hear;

but with righteousness he shall judge the poor,
and decide with equity for the meek of the earth;
and he shall smite the earth with the rod of his mouth,
and with the breath of his lips he shall slay the wicked.
(Is. 11:3-4)

Here is an utterly different picture. The Messiah is to rule;
he is to crush evil; he is to slay the wicked. How can such a
victorious ruler be at the same time the meek and lowly one
who pours out his soul in death (Is. 53:12)? This is why, in
spite of Isaiah 53, Jesus' disciples could not grasp the fact that
he must suffer and die. Messiah is to conquer and rule, not be
conquered and crushed. The Old Testament does not make it
clear that before Messiah is to come as conqueror and ruler,
he must first appear as the humble suffering servant.

A second fact is of equal importance. The suffering one is
never called Messiah or son of David. He is an unnamed individual. Furthermore, in its context, the suffering one is the
servant of the Lord *who is sometimes identified with Israel.* Isaiah
52:13—"Behold, my servant shall prosper"; Isaiah 50:10—
"Who among you fears the LORD and obeys the voice of his
servant?"; Isaiah 49:3—"You are my servant, Israel, in whom
I will be glorified"; Isaiah 49:5—"And now the LORD says,
who formed me from the womb to be his servant, to bring
Jacob back to him, and that Israel might be gathered to him";
Isaiah 45:3—"It is I, the LORD, the God of Israel, who call
you by name. For the sake of my servant Jacob, and Israel my
chosen."

In these references the servant is both Israel and one who
redeems Israel. There is an interplay between these two concepts. But in neither case is the servant called the Messiah or
the Davidic ruling king. Little wonder that it has been custom-
ary for Jewish exegetes to see in the servant not the conquering, delivering Messianic king, but the afflicted, suffering
people of Israel. Isaiah 53 is not, in its own historical setting,

a prophecy of Messiah. It becomes such only when it is interpreted in light of the Christ event.

This clearly establishes the principle that the "literal hermeneutic" does not work. For *literally*, Isaiah 53 is not a prophecy of Messiah but of an unnamed servant of the Lord. Old Testament prophecies must be interpreted in the light of the New Testament to find their deeper meaning.

This principle must be carried further. I do not see how it is possible to avoid the conclusion that the New Testament applies Old Testament prophecies to the New Testament church and in so doing identifies the church as spiritual Israel. I have come to this conclusion not because I read it in books or found it in some theological system, but from my own inductive study of the inspired Word of God.

A most vivid illustration of this principle is found in Romans 9 where Paul is talking about "us whom he has called, not from the Jews only but also from the Gentiles" (Rom. 9:24). In other words Paul is talking about the church in Rome which included some Jews but which was largely Gentile. To prove that it was God's purpose to call such a people into being, Paul quotes two passages from Hosea:

As indeed he says in Hosea,
"Those who were not my people
I will call 'my people,'
and her who was not beloved
I will call 'my beloved.' "
"And in the very place where it was said to them, 'You are
not my people,'
They will be called 'sons of the living God.' " (Rom. 9:25-26)
In Hosea both of the passages refer to literal, national Israel. Because of her rebelliousness, Israel is no longer the people of God. "And the LORD said, 'Call his name Not my people, for you are not my people and I am not your God' " (Hos. 1:9). Israel has been rejected by the Lord for her unbelief. Yet

Hosea sees a day of future repentance when a disobedient people will become obedient. He sees a large remnant, like the sand of the sea. "And in the place where it was said to them, 'You are not my people,' it shall be said to them, 'Sons of the living God' " (Hos. 1:10). This refers to a future conversion of the Jews. The same is true of the second prophecy: "And I will have pity on Not pitied, and I will say to Not my people, 'You are my people'; and he shall say, 'Thou art my God' " (Hos. 2:23). This again sees a future salvation of literal Israel when the people, whom God has rejected, will once again become the people of God.

Paul deliberately takes these two prophecies about the future salvation of Israel and applies them to the church. The church, consisting of both Jews and Gentiles, has become the people of God. The prophecies of Hosea are fulfilled in the Christian church. If this is a "spiritualizing hermeneutic," so be it. But let no one say that it is liberalism. It is clearly what the New Testament does to the Old Testament prophecies.

The idea of the Church as spiritual Israel is seen in other passages. Abraham is called "the father of all who believe" (Rom. 4:11); Abraham is "the father of us all" who "share the faith of Abraham" (Rom. 4:16); "It is men of faith who are the sons of Abraham" (Gal. 3:7); "And if you are Christ's, then you are Abraham's offspring, heirs according to promise" (Gal. 3:19). If Abraham is the father of a spiritual people, and if all believers are sons of Abraham, his offspring, then it follows that they are Israel, spiritually speaking.

This is what leads Paul to say, "For he is not a real Jew who is one outwardly, nor is true circumcision something external and physical. He is a Jew who is one inwardly, and real circumcision is a matter of the heart, spiritual and not literal" (Rom. 2:28-29). Now it is possible that in this verse Paul is speaking only of Jews, saying that a *true* Jew is not one who is only circumcised outwardly but who is also circumcised in the heart. He may not in these verses have Gentiles in view. But he clearly refers to the largely gentile church when he says to the Philippians, "For we are the true circumcision, who worship God in spirit, and glory in Christ Jesus" (Phil. 3:3).

Paul avoids calling the church Israel, unless it be in Galatians 6:16, but this is a much disputed verse. It is true, however, that he applies prophecies to the church which in their Old Testament setting belong to literal Israel; he calls the church the sons, the seeds of Abraham. He calls believers the true circumcision. It is difficult therefore to avoid the conclusion that Paul sees the church as spiritual Israel.

Another very important passage applies a prophecy given to Israel to the Christian church. In Jeremiah 31 the prophet foresees a day when God will make a new covenant with rebellious Israel. This new covenant will be characterized by a new work of God in the hearts of his people. "I will put my law within them, and I will write it upon their hearts; and I will be their God, and they shall be my people.... For they shall all know me, from the least of them to the greatest, says the LORD; for I will forgive their iniquity, and I will remember their sin no more" (Jer. 31:33-34).

The book of Hebrews applies this to the new covenant made in the blood of Christ. Hebrews 8 contrasts the new order introduced by Christ with the passing order of the Old Testament. Christ serves in the "true tent," not in the old, for the old is but "a copy and shadow of the heavenly sanctuary" (Heb. 8:5). Therefore Christ is the mediator of a new and better covenant, which rests on better promises (Heb. 8:6). "For if that first covenant had been faultless, there would have been no occasion for a second" (Heb. 8:7). These words make it clear that Hebrews is contrasting the old covenant which was defective with a second which has been established by Jesus. "For he finds fault with them ..." (Heb. 8:8), that is, God finds fault with Israel under the old order because they constantly broke the terms of the covenant. Therefore, a new covenant is necessary; and in describing this new covenant made by Christ, Hebrews 8:8-12 quotes Jeremiah 31:31-34. It seems impossible to avoid the conclusion that this quotation refers to the new covenant with the people of God—the Christian church—the new covenant which has been made possible because of the sacrifice of Christ.

Then, referring to the Old Testament cult, Hebrews concludes, "In speaking of a new covenant he treats the first as obsolete. And what is becoming obsolete and growing old is ready to vanish away" (Heb. 8:13). It is impossible to tell whether the temple in Jerusalem was still standing (it was destroyed in the Jewish War, A.D. 66-70), for the exact date of Hebrews is in doubt. But one thing is clear: Hebrews announces that the old order of the temple with its sacrifices is passé.

One of the central tenets of dispensational millennialism, based on its literal hermeneutic of the Old Testament prophecies, is that in the millennium, the Jewish temple will be rebuilt and the entire sacrificial system reinstituted, according to the prophecies of Ezekiel 40—48. However, there will be a difference between the millennial sacrifices and the Old Testament sacrifices. The millennial sacrifices will be a memorial to the sacrificial death of Jesus. "Those who consider the millennial sacrifices as a ritual which will be literally observed in the millennium invest the sacrifices with the central meaning of a memorial looking back to the one offering of Christ."[7] Any idea of a restoration of the Old Testament sacrificial systems, whether memorial or otherwise, stands in direct opposition to Hebrews 8:13, which unambiguously affirms that the Old Testament cult is both obsolete and about to pass away.

Therefore Hebrews 8:8-13 refutes dispensational theology at two points: It applies a prophecy to the Christian church which in its Old Testament setting referred to Israel, and it affirms that the new covenant in Christ has displaced the Old Testament cult which is therefore doomed to pass away.

The main point in the preceding section is that many Old Testament passages which applied in their historical setting to literal Israel have in the New Testament been applied to the church. What does all this have to do with the question of the millennium? Just this: The Old Testament did not clearly foresee how its own prophecies were to be fulfilled. They were fulfilled in ways quite unforeseen by the Old Testament itself and unexpected by the Jews. With regard to the first coming of Christ, *the Old Testament is interpreted by the New Testament.*

Here is the basic watershed between a dispensational and a nondispensational theology. Dispensationalism forms its eschatology by a literal interpretation of the Old Testament and then fits the New Testament into it. A nondispensational eschatology forms its theology from the explicit teaching of the New Testament. It confesses that it cannot be sure how the Old Testament prophecies of the end are to be fulfilled, for (a) the first coming of Christ was accomplished in terms not foreseen by a literal interpretation of the Old Testament, and (b) there are unavoidable indications that the Old Testament promises to Israel are fulfilled in the Christian church.

The alert reader will say, "This sounds like amillennialism." And so it does. I suspect that the amillennial writer will heartily agree with all that has been said thus far. However, there are two passages in the New Testament which cannot be avoided. One is Romans 11:26: "And so all Israel will be saved." It is difficult to escape the conclusion that this means literal Israel.

Paul has used the figure of the olive tree—the people of God. Israel is the natural branches; Gentiles are the wild branches. Contrary to nature, wild branches have been grafted with the tree, while natural branches, Israel, have been broken off because of unbelief (Rom. 11:19). However, the natural branches will be regrafted into their own tree if they do not continue in unbelief (Rom. 11:23). If wild branches have been grafted into the tree contrary to nature, "how much more will these natural branches be grafted back into their own olive tree" (Rom. 11:24). This is the context of Paul's statement, that a hardening has come upon (a large) part of Israel until the full number of the Gentiles comes in. "And so [that is, in this way, after a period of hardening] all Israel will be saved" (Rom. 11:26).

While the New Testament clearly affirms the salvation of literal Israel, it does not give any details about the day of salvation. This, however, must be said: Israel's salvation must occur in the same terms as Gentile salvation, by faith in Jesus as their crucified Messiah. As we have already pointed out, New Testament exegesis (Hebrews 8) makes it difficult to believe that the Old Testament prophecies about the "millennial temple" will be fulfilled literally. They are fulfilled in the New Covenant established in the blood of Jesus. It may well be that Israel's conversion will take place in connection with the millennium. It may be that in the millennium, for the first time in human history, we will witness a truly Christian nation. However, the New Testament does not give any details of Israel's conversion and role in the millennium. So a nondispensational eschatology simply affirms the future salvation of Israel and remains open to God's future as to the details.

It by no means follows, as some amillennialists argue, that because many of the Old Testament promises are fulfilled in the church, this is to be taken as a single normative principle and that *all* of the promises to Israel are fulfilled in the church without exception. We have already sought to prove that the New Testament teaches the final salvation of Israel. Israel remains the elect people of God, a "holy" people (Rom. 11:16). We cannot know how the Old Testament prophecies will be fulfilled, except to say that Israel remains the people of God and will yet experience a divine visitation which will result in her salvation.

The Context of Millennialism
A second consideration is equally important. Any millennial doctrine must be consistent with its New Testament context, particularly its Christology.

One of the central doctrines of the New Testament, often neglected, is that of the heavenly session of Christ. "When he had made purification for sins, he sat down at the right hand of the Majesty on high" (Heb. 1:3). This is a theme which is often reiterated in the New Testament. "Thou hast crowned him with glory and honor, putting everything in subjection under his feet" (Heb. 2:7-8). "But when Christ had offered for all time a single sacrifice for sins, he sat down at the right hand of God, then to wait until his enemies should be made a stool for his feet" (Heb. 10:12-13).

Here we have a clear allusion to Psalm 110:1: "The LORD says to my lord: 'Sit at my right hand, till I make your enemies your footstool.'" The right hand is the place of preference, the place of power, the place of pre-eminence. This has to do with Christ's reign as Messianic King. The right hand is in effect the throne of God. "He who conquers, I will grant him to sit with me on my throne, as I myself conquered and sat down with my Father on his throne" (Rev. 3:21). Christ is now reigning from heaven as God's vice regent. The reign of Christ has as its goal the subjugation of every hostile power. "Then comes the end, when he delivers the kingdom to God the Father after destroying every rule and every authority and power. For he must reign until he has put all his enemies under his feet. The last enemy to be destroyed is death" (1 Cor. 15:24-26). The New Testament does not make the reign of Christ one that is limited to Israel in the millennium.

It is a spiritual reign in heaven which has already been inaugurated, and its primary purpose is to destroy Christ's spiritual enemies, the last of which is death.

The truth of the present exaltation and reign of Christ is clearly expressed in the great Christological passage—Philippians 2:5-10. Although he existed in the form of God, Christ did not consider equality with God a thing to be grasped, as Adam had tried to do. Rather, he poured himself out by taking the form of a slave and was born in the likeness of men. Being found in human form, he humbled himself by becoming obedient to death, even the death of a cross. This is why God has highly exalted him and has given to Jesus the title and status of *Lord*. The goal is that at the name of Jesus, every knee shall bow and every tongue confess that *Jesus Christ is Lord* to the glory of God the Father.

The primary primitive Christian confession was not of Jesus as Savior but of Jesus as Lord. "If you confess with your lips that Jesus is Lord and believe in your heart that God raised him from the dead, you will be saved" (Rom. 10:9). This is more than a confession that Jesus is *my* Lord. It is first a theological confession that I recognize that God has exalted Jesus to the status of Lord. He *is* the Lord; he has been exalted to God's right hand. Therefore, I make him *my* Lord by bowing to his sovereignty.

Lordship and kingship are interchangeable terms. This is seen in 1 Timothy 6:15. God is our "blessed and only Sovereign, the King of kings and Lord of lords." While this verse speaks of the Father, it is by the mediatorial work of the Lord Jesus that every enemy shall be put beneath his feet. When this has been accomplished and he has destroyed "every rule and every authority and power," Jesus the Lord will deliver the *kingdom* to God the Father (1 Cor. 15:24). "When all things are subjected to him, then the Son himself will also be subjected to him who put all things under him, that God may be everything to every one" (1 Cor. 15:28).

The same truth is clearly set forth in Peter's Pentecost address which he concludes with the statement, "Let all the house of Israel therefore know assuredly that God has made him both Lord and Christ, this Jesus whom you crucified" (Acts 2:36). Taken out of context, this verse might mean that Jesus *became* Lord and Christ at his exaltation. However, Acts 3:18 makes it clear that it was as the Christ that Jesus endured his sufferings. Therefore the verse means that in his exaltation, Jesus entered a new stage of his Messianic mission. *Christ* means "anointed one" and refers to his role as the anointed Davidic King. Lord is a religious word meaning absolute sovereign.

The significance of this saying is seen in Peter's sermon. David knew that God had sworn to set one of his—David's—descendents upon his throne. Therefore he foresaw and spoke of the resurrection of Christ. He has been exalted at the right hand of God. "For David did not ascend into the heavens; but he himself says, 'The Lord said to my Lord, Sit at my right hand, till I make thy enemies a stool for thy feet' " (Acts 2:34-35). Here again is the quotation from Psalm 110. Again it is difficult to avoid the conclusion that Peter means that in Jesus' exaltation and session at the right hand of God, God has fulfilled the promise of Psalm 110. Peter, under inspiration, has transferred the throne of David from Jerusalem —Zion (Ps. 110:2)—to heaven. In his session Jesus has been made Lord. He has also begun his reign as the Messianic, Davidic King. He has entered upon his reign as Lord and Christ.

This truth is reflected in one of the three Greek words used to designate the Second Coming of Jesus: *apokalypsis*, which means "revelation." Paul tells the Corinthians that they are awaiting "the revealing of our Lord Jesus Christ" (1 Cor. 1:7). The return of the Lord will mean rest for afflicted Christians "when the Lord Jesus is revealed from heaven" (2 Thess. 1:7). The Second Coming of Christ will mean nothing less than the disclosure to the world of the sovereignty and lordship which is already his. He is *now* the Lord; he is *now* reigning at the right hand of God. However, his present reign is seen only by the eye of faith. It is unseen and unrecognized by the world. His second advent will mean the unveiling—the revelation— the disclosure of the lordship which is already his. It will mean "the appearing of the glory of our great God and Savior Jesus Christ" (Tit. 2:13).

We cannot find warrant in the Scripture for the idea that Jesus is Lord of the church while the King of Israel. We do not find in Scripture the idea that Jesus begins his Messianic reign at his parousia and that his kingship belongs primarily to the millennium. We find on the contrary that the millennial reign of Christ will be the manifestation in history of the lordship and sovereignty which is his already.

Millennialism
We must now turn to the New Testament to study its teachings about a millennium. For reasons outlined above, a millennial doctrine cannot be based on Old Testament prophecies but should be based on the New Testament alone.

The only place in the Bible that speaks of an actual millennium is the passage in Revelation 20:1-6. Any millennial doctrine must be based upon the most natural exegesis of this passage.

The book of Revelation belongs to the genre of literature called apocalyptic. The first apocalyptic book was the canonical Daniel. This was followed by a large group of imitative apocalypses between 200 B.C. and A.D. 100 such as Enoch, Assumption of Moses, 4 Ezra, and the Apocalypse of Baruch. Two facts emerge from the study of apocalyptic: The apocalypses use highly symbolic language to describe a series of events in history; and the main concern of apocalyptic is the end of the age and the establishment of God's kingdom. Sometimes there is a Messiah but not always. In the Assumption of Moses, it is God himself who establishes his kingdom.[8] To illustrate: Daniel sees four beasts rise out of the sea which represent a succession of four worldwide empires. Then he sees one like a son of man come to the throne of God, receive a kingdom which he brings to earth to the saints of the Most High (Dan. 2). This is Daniel's way of describing the end of the age and the establishment of God's kingdom.

In the Revelation of John the beast of chapter 13 is both the Rome of ancient history and an eschatological Antichrist.[9] The first thing to note is that the events of Revelation 20 follow the vision of the Second Coming of Christ, which is pictured in 19:11-16. In this vision the emphasis is altogether on the coming of Christ as the Conqueror. He is pictured as riding on a white horse like a warrior, accompanied by the armies of heaven. He comes as "King of kings and Lord of lords" (Rev. 19:16). He comes to do battle with Antichrist, who has been pictured in chapters 13 and 17. It is noteworthy that the only weapon mentioned is the sword that proceeds from his mouth. With it he smites the nations (Rev. 19:15). Here is a marvel indeed. He wins his victories by his word alone, which is "living and active, sharper than any two-edged sword" (Heb. 4:12). He will not win his victory by the use of the military weapons of the world but with his bare word. He will speak and the victory will be his.

Some systems of interpretation do not see in this vision the Second Coming of Christ. Rather they see a highly symbolic portrayal of the witness of the Word of God in the world through the church. This interpretation seems impossible. The theme of the Revelation is the return of the Lord to consummate his redemptive work. "Behold, he is coming with the clouds, and every eye will see him, every one who pierced him;

and all the tribes of the earth will wail on account of him" (Rev. 1:7). We cannot here review the role the Second Coming of Christ plays in New Testament theology as a whole. It can only be said that it is an absolutely central doctrine in every portion of the New Testament. The Incarnation was a divine invasion into history in which the divine majesty and glory were veiled in Jesus' humanity. The Second Coming will be a second divine invasion in which the majesty and glory of God will be revealed. Revelation 19 is the only passage in the Revelation which describes the Second Coming of Christ. If this passage be interpreted differently, the Revelation nowhere describes the return of the Lord.

Furthermore, Revelation 19:6-10 announces the "marriage of the Lamb"—the union of Christ with his bride, the church, which will occur at Christ's return. The marriage itself is not described; it takes place at the return of the Lord. The theme is mentioned again in 21:2 where the heavenly Jerusalem, representing the redeemed people of God, is seen coming down from heaven, "prepared as a bride adorned for her husband." Jesus used the metaphor of a wedding feast to describe the eschatological coming of the kingdom (Mt. 22: 1-14), and he likened the unknown hour of the coming of the kingdom to the uncertain hour of the coming of the bridegroom (Mt. 25:1-13). Paul likens the relationship of the church to Christ to that of a "pure bride [virgin] to her one husband" (2 Cor. 11:2). Here, the church is not yet the wife; the marriage is the eschatological union. Again Paul likens the relationship of Christ and his church to that of a husband and his wife (Eph. 5:25-33), but the actual wedding is viewed as future when the church is presented before him "in splendor, without spot or wrinkle or any such thing, that she might be holy and without blemish" (Eph. 5:27). In the Revelation the actual event of the wedding is nowhere described; it is a metaphorical way of alluding to the final redemptive act when "the dwelling of God is with men. He will dwell with them, and they shall be his people, and God himself will be with them" (Rev. 21:3).

Chapters 19—20 form a continuous narrative announcing the marriage of the Lamb, the victorious return of Christ and his victory over his enemies. Revelation 19:17-21 describes in terms of ancient warfare Christ's victory over the beast and the false prophet: "These two were thrown alive into the lake of fire that burns with sulphur" (19:20). Chapter 20 relates Christ's victory over the one who stood behind the beast, the devil. The victory over the devil occurs in two stages. First, he is bound and shut up in the "bottomless pit" for a thousand years, "that he should deceive the nations no more" (Rev. 20:3), as he had done through the beast. Only at the end of the thousand years is Satan finally cast into the lake of fire and brimstone to share the fate of the beast and the false prophet (20:10).

This is to me the only admissible exegesis of Revelation 20:1-6. The exegesis of the passage depends upon one's interpretation of verses 4-5: "They [the persons mentioned earlier in v. 4] came to life, and reigned with Christ a thousand years. The rest of the dead did not come to life until the thousand years were ended. This is the first resurrection." The Greek behind the translation "they come to life" is a single verb, *ezēsan*, which could also be translated "they lived." What does it mean "to live"? The entire interpretation of the passage hinges upon the question of whether the first *ezēsan* and the *ezēsan* of the rest of the dead mean the same thing, namely, bodily resurrection. What is the "first resurrection"? Is it literal, a resurrection of the body, or spiritual, a resurrection of the soul? If we can find the answer to this question, we shall have the key to the solution of the millennial question in this passage.

The "spiritual" interpretation of the first *ezēsan* cannot be objected to on the grounds that the New Testament does not teach any spiritual resurrection, for it clearly does. Ephesians 2:1-6 teaches that we, who once were dead in sins, have been made alive and have been raised from the dead with Jesus Christ. This is clearly a resurrection of the spirit which occurs when one comes to faith in Jesus Christ.

Again, in John 5:25-29, spiritual resurrection and bodily resurrection occur in the same context:

Truly, truly I say unto you, the hour is coming, and now is, when the dead will hear the voice of the Son of God, and those who hear will live [*zesousin*]. . . . Do not marvel at this; for the hour is coming when all who are in the tombs will hear his voice and come forth, those who have done good, to the resurrection of life, and those who have done evil, to the resurrection of judgment.

Here is first a spiritual resurrection, to be followed by an eschatological bodily resurrection. Nonmillenarian interpreters argue that Revelation 20 should be interpreted in a way analogous to John 5.

This passage does not provide a real analogy to the passage in the Apocalypse, however. There is this all-important difference. In John the context itself provides the clues for the spiritual interpretation in the one instance and the literal in the other. Concerning the first group who live, *the hour has already come.* This makes it clear that it refers to those who are spiritually dead and who enter into life upon hearing the voice of the Son of God. The second group, however, are *in the tombs.* They are not spiritually dead but physically dead. Such dead are to be brought back to life again. Part of them will experience a "resurrection of life," a bodily resurrection into the eternal life of the Age to Come. The rest will be raised to a "resurrection of condemnation," to the execution of the decree of divine judgment which rests upon them because they have rejected the Son of God and the life he came to bring

(John 3:18, 36). The language of these words makes it indubitable that Jesus wishes his hearers to know that he is speaking of two kinds of "living": a present spiritual resurrection and a future bodily resurrection.

In Revelation 20 *there is no such contextual clue for a similar variation of interpretation.* The language of the passage is quite clear and unambiguous. There is neither necessity nor con textual possibility to interpret either *ezēsan* spiritually in order to introduce meaning to the passage. At the beginning of the thousand years some of the dead come to life; at the conclusion, the rest of the dead come to life. There is no evident play upon words here. The passage makes perfectly good sense when interpreted literally.

This is reinforced by the fact that the same word is used in reference to coming to life twice elsewhere in the Revelation. In Revelation 2:8 we read, "The words of the first and the last, who died and came to life" (*ezēsan*). Here is a clear reference to the resurrection of Jesus. In 13:14 we read of the beast "who was wounded by the sword and yet lived" (*ezēsan*). From 13:3, we know that the wound was "a mortal wound," a wound unto death.

We must conclude that such passages as Ephesians 2 and John 5 are not truly analogous to Revelation 20 and do not provide sufficient justification for interpreting the first *ezēsan* spiritually and the second literally. Natural inductive exegesis suggests that both words are to be taken in the same way, referring to literal resurrection. We can do no better than to repeat the oft-quoted words of Henry Alford:

> If, in a passage where *two resurrections* are mentioned, where certain *psychai ezēsan* at the first, and the rest of the *nekroi ezēsan* only at the end of a specified period after the first,— if in such a passage the first resurrection may be understood to mean *spiritual* rising with Christ, while the second means literal rising from the grave;—then there is an end of

all significance in language, and Scripture is wiped out as a definite testimony to anything.[10]

Some emphasize the fact that what John saw was *psychai*— souls, not bodies. This is not quite true. John saw *psychai* which *ezēsan*—which come to life in resurrection.

The strongest objection to millennialism is that this truth is found in only one passage of Scripture—Revelation 20. Non-millenarians appeal to the argument of analogy, that difficult passages must be interpreted by clear passages. It is a fact that most of the New Testament writings say nothing about a millennium.

One of the most important "millennial" passages in the Gospels for dispensationalists is the parable of the sheep and the goats in Matthew 25:31-46. We are told that this is the judgment to determine who enters the millennium and who is excluded. This is impossible for the text itself says that the righteous will go away into eternal life while the wicked go into eternal punishment (Mt. 25:46). "Eternal life" is not the millennium but the eternal life of the Age to Come. Indeed, Dr. John Walvoord labels me an amillennialist because I do not find the millennium in such passages.[11] I can find no trace of the idea of either an interim earthly kingdom or of a millennium in the Gospels.[12]

There is, however, one passage in Paul which may refer to an interim kingdom if not a millennium. In 1 Corinthians 15:23-26 Paul pictures the triumph of Christ's kingdom as being accomplished in several stages. The resurrection of Christ is the first stage (*tagma*). The second stage will occur at the parousia when those who are Christ's will share his resurrection. "Then comes the end, when he delivers the kingdom to God the Father after destroying every rule and every authority and power. For he must reign until he has put all his enemies under his feet. The last enemy to be destroyed is death." The adverbs translated "then" are *epeita*,

eita, which denote a sequence: "after that." There are three distinct stages: Jesus' resurrection; after that (*epeita*) the resurrection of believers at the resurrection; after that (*eita*) the end (*telos*). An unidentified interval falls between Christ's resurrection and his parousia, and a second undefined interval falls between the parousia and the *telos*, when Christ completes the subjugation of his enemies.[13]

We have here an instance of progressive revelation. The main purpose of prophecy is not to answer all our questions about the future but to enable God's people to live in the present in light of the future (2 Pet. 1:19). Evangelicals who believe the Bible to be God's Word containing God's revelation to humanity recognize progressive revelation. It should not trouble us that the New Testament for the most part does not foresee the millennial kingdom any more than the fact that the Old Testament does not clearly predict the Church Age.

The New Testament nowhere expounds the theology of the millennium, that is, its purpose in God's redemptive plan. In some way not disclosed in Scripture, the millennium is part of Christ's Messianic rule by which he puts all his enemies under his feet (1 Cor. 15:25). Another possible role of the millennium is that Christ's Messianic kingdom might be disclosed *in history*. The purpose of Jesus' earthly ministry was to bring God's kingdom to men (Mt. 12:28). Because the King has come, we have already been delivered from the power of darkness and transferred into his kingdom (Col. 1:13). We have argued above that Christ began his Messianic reign at his resurrection-ascension; but his present reign is invisible, unseen and unrecognized by the world, visible only to the eye of faith. The order of the Age to Come will involve a new heaven and a new earth, and will be so different from the present order that we can speak of it as *beyond history* (2 Pet. 3:12; Rev. 21—22). The millennium will reveal to the world as we now know it the glory and power of Christ's reign.

There is another possible reason for Christ's millennial reign. At its close the devil will be released from his imprisonment and will find the hearts of men still responsive to his enticements, even though they have lived in a period of peace and righteousness. This will serve to commend the justice of God in the final judgment. Sin—rebellion against God—is not due to an evil society or to a bad environment. It is due to the sinfulness of the hearts of men. Thus the justice of God will be fully vindicated in the day of final judgment.

There are admittedly serious theological problems with the doctrine of a millennium. However, even if theology cannot find an answer for all its questions, evangelical theology must build upon the clear teaching of Scripture. Therefore I am a premillennialist.

A DISPENSATIONAL PREMILLENNIAL RESPONSE
HERMAN A. HOYT

The presentation of each of the millennial views in this book centers on the hermeneutic or principle of interpretation adopted by each writer. This principle of interpretation develops a system of theology that makes it almost impossible for each writer to see anything that conflicts with or falls outside the system. When the writer finds himself in tight quarters, he either ignores the issues or engages in some sort of rationalization to make the circumstances fit the system. This is greater or lesser depending upon the viewpoint of the writer, and in every case the sincerity of the writer may be unquestioned. Each believes his system is the least subject to inadequacies, and Ladd, along with the others, believes this is true of his system.

Reference to "historic" premillennialism suggests something that I do not believe is true. The fathers of the church from the second century on have not held this view, and this therefore does not establish its validity. Any fundamental validity that is truly historic is to be found in the New Testament—something that was espoused by the early church and persisted for several hundred years.

Ladd is right in introducing his discussion of the subject of millennialism with "The Question of Hermeneutics." In his introductory paragraphs, his principle of interpretation leads him to make one observation that excludes any other view. He believes that the church will not be raptured until after the tribulation. The reference to the "first resurrection" (Rev. 20:5) must mean that all the companies of the saved are resurrected at the same time. It is the dispensational view that the *final* company of the saved is resurrected at this time, thus completing the first resurrection.

It is very clear from Ladd's discussion of hermeneutics that he is decidedly opposed to the dispensational system. Yet I find it hard to understand why one system is labeled dispensational and others escape that description. For the facts are these: Not one view of the millennium in this book is without some arrangement of dispensations; it is impossible to interpret the Bible apart from some arrangement of dispensations; and most certainly the very mention of an eschatological millennium imposes another dispensation. But it is clear that Ladd can find no place for any system of dispensations other than his own and that the chief difficulty for him lies in the emphasis upon literal interpretation of Scripture endorsed by those known as "dispensationalists."

Ladd is conscious of the fact that literal interpretation is the cornerstone of dispensational millennialism. "Old Testament prophecies must be interpreted literally" (p. 18). This helps to draw clear distinctions between the nation of Israel and the Christian church. But he refuses to understand that the Old Testament is not complete apart from the New Testament and that the New Testament cannot be comprehended apart from the Old Testament. By his own admission he insists that the New Testament interprets the Old. There is certainly a measure of truth on this point. But in passage after passage Ladd insists that the New Testament is interpreting the Old when the New Testament is simply applying a principle found in the Old Testament (Hos. 11:1 with Mt. 2:15; Hos. 1:10; 2:23 with Rom. 9:24-26). Rushing to the conclusion that these references identify the church and Israel as the same body of the saved is wholly gratuitous. Even though "the New Testament applies Old Testament prophecies to the New Testament church" (p. 23), it does not do so in the sense of identifying the church as spiritual Israel. It makes such application merely for the purpose of explaining something that is true of both.

Zeroing in on the central issue at stake, Ladd asserts: "Dispensationalism forms its eschatology by a literal interpretation of the Old Testament and then fits the New Testament into it. A nondispensational eschatology forms its theology from the explicit teaching of the New Testament" (p. 27). In my judgment this is not a fair statement of the facts. The dispensationalist interprets the New Testament in the light of the Old, whereas the nondispensationalist, it seems, comes to the New Testament with a system of interpretation which is not derived from the Old Testament and superimposes this upon the New Testament. When Ladd affirms that "(a) the first coming of Christ was accomplished in terms not foreseen by a literal interpretation of the Old Testament, and (b) there are unavoidable indications that the Old Testament promises to Israel are fulfilled in the Christian church" (p. 27), it not only sounds like amillennialism, it comes close to being amillennialism. To escape this indictment he finds it necessary to shift from spiritualization to literalism in interpreting such passages as Romans 11 where the church is clearly distinguished from Israel.

As Ladd passes from interpretation to the context of millennialism, he is concerned to be consistent with New Testament Christology. He insists that Christ is now exalted to the high position of Lord and Christ, is exercising his power, and is reigning from heaven as God's vice regent. There may be dispensationalists who will play on the words of Lord and King and find distinctions which possess no real difference— confining Lord to the church and King to the millennium— but in any such case this is a mere fringe so far as dispensationalism is concerned. The core of dispensationalism will follow the point made by Ladd: In the millennium there will be a revelation of Christ as sovereign whose rule during the millennium will progressively bring every enemy into subjection to him, the last one being death (1 Cor. 15:24-26). During the millennium Christ will rule over all the earth including Gentiles as well as Israel. But this rule, contrary to Ladd's view, will be in direct relation to the earth. This rule will be personal, earthly, visible, real and spiritual.

Concluding his remarks, Ladd declares that very little is set forth in the New Testament on the millennium and that one passage alone contains practically all that is revealed. He refers to Revelation 19—20. But this is probably an understatement to which even Ladd would agree. From other portions of the New Testament other details greatly enhance the picture. It is unfortunate that he cannot see that the Old Testament supplies the vast portion of material for putting the picture in full perspective.

Ladd is quite right in insisting that Revelation 19—20 marks the grand climax of the ministry of Christ in his Second Coming. "Behold, he is coming with the clouds, and every eye will see him, everyone who pierced him; and all tribes of the earth will wail on account of him" (Rev. 1:7). This includes the marriage of the Lamb to the bride (the church), the defeat of the mobilized armies under Antichrist and the casting of the two evil geniuses into the lake of fire. Then there is the incarceration of Satan in the bottomless pit for the thousand years. At this point there is physical resurrection of saints. After the thousand years comes the resurrection of the wicked, their judgment and the ushering in of the eternal state.

It is heartening to find Ladd sticking to contextual and literal exegesis in dealing with the resurrections of chapter 20. At this point he cites a long passage from Henry Alford in support of this method of interpretation. As Ladd points out, there is a progressive triumph of Christ's kingdom as set forth in 1 Corinthians 15:23-26, in which Christ completes the subjugation of his enemies. The first stage is marked by the resurrection of Christ himself. This is followed by an undefined period of time, the Church Age. Then comes the parousia and the resurrection of the saved. This is followed by another period undefined by 1 Corinthians 15, which is defined in Revelation 20 as the millennial kingdom. The third stage is the end when Christ will raise the wicked dead and judge them, and then turn the kingdom over to the Father for eternity.

Even though Ladd asserts that the New Testament revelation concerning the millennium is limited, he is right in pointing out that there is sufficient material to note a progressive revelation. By no means are all the questions answered. But one underlying purpose can be discerned, namely, practical value "to enable God's people to live in the present in light of the future (2 Pet. 1:19)" (p. 39). Nowhere in any formal sense does the New Testament expound the theology of the millennium. But men are made aware of the fact that there is a new order of revelation and control during the kingdom. After a thousand years in an almost perfect environment, it will become clear that "sin—rebellion against God—is not due to an evil society or to a bad environment. It is due to the sinfulness of the hearts of men" (p. 40).

After moving through the entire doctrine of the millennium with attendant truth, Ladd does what every other writer in this volume does explicitly or implicitly, namely, admits there are serious theological problems with the doctrine of the millennium. The student of Scripture is confined to revelation, and not all the problems are resolved there. So he does his best with the material at hand. This has led Ladd to affirm, "Therefore I am a premillennialist."

A POSTMILLENNIAL RESPONSE
LORAINE BOETTNER

I am favorably impressed with Ladd's discussion of the manner in which Old Testament prophecy is interpreted and applied by the New Testament. His treatment seems to me essentially correct. He shows that whereas dispensationalism holds that the church was not foreseen by the Old Testament prophets and that it was established only as a kind of secondary measure after the kingdom Christ offered the Jews had been rejected, it is hard to avoid the conclusion that "the New Testament applies Old Testament prophecies to the New Testament church and in so doing identifies the church as spiritual Israel" (p. 23). He also shows that the "basic watershed" between dispensational and nondispensational theology is that "dispensationalism forms its eschatology by a literal interpretation of the Old Testament and then fits the New Testament into it" while "a nondispensational eschatology forms its theology from the explicit teaching of the New Testament" (p. 27). But I do differ quite radically with his view of the millennium derived from Revelation 20:1-6. However, Hoekema has discussed Revelation 20:1-6, and I refer the reader to pages 159-72 for what seems to me a satisfactory analysis.

I should like to limit my discussion primarily to the differences that exist regarding the conversion of the Jews and the position that they are yet to have in this present world and in the millennial kingdom. Ladd quotes Rom. 11:26 ("and so all Israel shall be saved") and concludes that the verse means literal Israel. He says that "we cannot know how the Old Testament prophecies will be fulfilled, except to say that Israel remains the people of God and will yet experience a divine visitation which will result in her salvation" (pp. 28-29). He adds, however, and surely quite correctly, that "Israel's salvation must occur in the same terms as Gentile salvation, by faith in Jesus as their crucified Messiah" (p. 28).

Ladd acknowledges that "a millennial doctrine cannot be based on Old Testament prophecies but should be based on the New Testament alone," and that "the only place in the Bible that speaks of an actual millennium is the passage in Revelation 20:1-6" (p. 32). He says that "Christ is now reigning from heaven as God's vice regent" (p. 29). He quotes Hebrews 1:3: "When he had made purification for sins, he sat down at the right hand of the Majesty on high," and says that Christ is now seated at the right hand of God, which is the position of power and pre-eminence. In fulfillment of Psalm 110:1, Christ is to occupy that position until his enemies have been made his footstool. This means that Christ "is *now* the Lord; he is *now* reigning at the right hand of God. However, his present reign is seen only by the eye of faith. It is unseen and unrecognized by the world. His second advent will mean the unveiling—the revelation—the disclosure of the lordship which is already his." I think that is correct. In fact those words might well have been written by an amillennialist or a postmillennialist. But as a postmillennialist I miss any emphasis on the result of that reign toward the winning of the world for righteousness during the Church Age.

Ladd has very little to say about the nature of the millennial reign of Christ over the earth. He says, "The New Testament nowhere expounds the theology of the millennium, that is, its purpose in God's redemptive plan. In some way not disclosed in Scripture, the millennium is part of Christ's Messianic rule by which he puts all his enemies under his feet (1 Cor. 15:25)" (p. 39). He does say that Israel is to be converted, and that "in the millennium for the first time in human history, we will witness a truly Christian nation." And he adds, "The New Testament does not give any details of Israel's conversion and role in the millennium. So a nondispensational eschatology simply affirms the future salvation of Israel and remains open to God's future as to the details" (p. 28).

While Ladd does not attempt any explanation, a curious situation surely does arise when Christ and the resurrected and translated saints return to earth to set up the millennial kingdom in association with men still in the flesh. That condition, semiheavenly and semiearthly, with Christ reigning—apparently—in Jerusalem, with two radically different types of people (the saints in glorified, resurrected bodies and ordinary mortals still in the flesh mingling freely throughout the world for the long and almost unending period of one thousand years) strikes me as so unreal and impossible that I wonder how anyone can take it seriously. Such a mixed state of mortals and immortals, terrestrial and celestial, surely would be a monstrosity. It would be as incongruous as for the holy angels now to mingle in their work and pleasure and worship with the present population of the world, bringing heavenly splendor into a sinful environment. Exalt the millennium as you please, it still remains far below heaven. It could not be other than a great anticlimax for those who have tasted of the heavenly glory to be brought back again to have a part in this life. Such positions of authority and rulership as might be given to them in this world would be a poor compensation for the glory that they have enjoyed in heaven.

In developing their ideas of what conditions will be like during the millennium, premillennialists fail to take into consideration the overpowering majesty of the risen and glorified Christ. They imagine that men will be in personal contact with him as he reigns from an earthly throne. Apparently they assume that he will be as he was in the days of his humiliation. But when the ascended and glorified Christ appeared to Saul on the road to Damascus, Saul was stricken blind by the light and fell to the ground. When the Apostle John saw him, "his face was like the sun shining in full strength." And, John says, "When I saw him, I fell at his feet as though dead" (Rev. 1: 16-17). If such glory was so overpowering that the beloved disciple John fell at his feet as though dead, how much less shall ordinary mortals, sinners, be able to stand before him! Paul described him as "the blessed and only sovereign, the King of kings and Lord of lords, who only has immortality and dwells in unapproachable light, whom no man has ever seen or can see" (1 Tim. 6:15-16).

When Christ returns in his own glory and that of the Father, with all the holy angels, certainly no mere man, who by comparison is but a worm of the dust, shall be able to stand before him. His period of humiliation is over, and his divine glory forbids the approach of those who are tainted with sin. No mortal man can come into that presence and not be overwhelmed by it. That vision is reserved for heaven. This world and the people in it cannot stand such glory.

The idea of a provisional kingdom in which glorified saints and mortal men mingle finds no support anywhere in Scripture. When the saints are caught up to meet the Lord in the air, it is said, "So we shall always be with the Lord" (1 Thess. 4:17). There is no hint of coming back to the earth before the time of the new heaven and the new earth of the eternal state. Our natural bodies cannot enter the heavenly kingdom, and we may be sure that the resurrection bodies of the saints would be equally out of place if brought back to live again in this environment. Once the saints have passed through the portals of death and have received their resurrection bodies, they have attained a state far too exalted for any earthly millennium. Regardless of how attractively the millennial state may be pictured, those who have been nourished on the first fruits of heavenly life can never again find earthly life attractive or significant. The heavenly bliss that the saints enjoy is incomparably superior to even the most glowing representation of any earthly life that can be imagined.

On the basis of Romans 11:26, "And so all Israel will be saved," Ladd holds that Israel will be converted, probably in connection with the millennium. But this verse has been subject to various interpretations. Paul's teaching in other places does not support that view. In Galatians 3:7 he says, "It is men of faith who are the sons of Abraham"; and again, "There is neither Jew nor Greek, there is neither slave nor free, there is neither male nor female, for you are all one in Christ Jesus. And if you are Christ's, then you are Abraham's offspring, heirs according to promise" (Gal. 2:28-29). He says that Christ has broken down the "dividing wall of hostility" between Jews and Gentiles, that he "might reconcile us both to God in one body through the cross" (Eph. 2:14-16). He refers to New Testament believers as "the Israel of God" (Gal. 6:16). His teaching is that in matters of faith the spiritual relationship takes precedence over the physical and that all true believers are sons of Abraham. And conversely we may say that those who are not true believers are not sons of Abraham in any sense worthy of the name, regardless of what their ancestry may be. Paul uses strong words to assert his teaching on this subject. How could you express more positively that the old distinction between Jew and Gentile has been wiped out? In the church there are no promises or privileges given to any one group or nationality which do not apply equally to all others.

Concerning the nation of Israel itself, when Christ came
and was rejected, he deposed the leaders of apostate Judaism,
the Pharisees and elders, and appointed a new set of officials,
the apostles, through whom he would establish his church. To
the rulers of Judaism he said, "The kingdom of God will be
taken away from you and given to a nation [the church] producing the fruits of it" (Mt. 21:43). And because of their sin in
rejecting and crucifying the Messiah, they were brought into
a position in which, as Paul says, "God's wrath has come upon
them at last" (1 Thess. 2:16). In accordance with this the entire
system of Judaism has been abrogated, brought to an end and
abolished. And in its place the New Covenant has become the
authoritative and official instrument for God's dealings with
his people, the church.

The assumption of modern premillennialism that God still
has a special purpose to be served by the Jewish people as a
nation proceeds on the false notion that they are in themselves
a people divinely favored above all others in the world, that
they are to be blessed for their own sake because they are Jews
—and all this in spite of being the most bitter enemies of the
church for the last two thousand years. Originally there was
reason for the selection of a particular people. God's plan of
salvation for a lost world was that he would provide a Redeemer through whose life and death redemption would be
worked out. It was necessary that a particular group of people, or nation, be set aside to prepare the way for and to bring
the Messiah into the world. Originally the choice was confined
to one individual, Abraham, whose seed was to develop into
that nation. Until the work of redemption was accomplished
that nation would be kept separate from all the other nations
which were completely given over to heathenism.

Because of that choice, the Jewish nation became the exclu-
sive channel through which God chose to reveal himself to the
world. But now that the Messiah has come and God's revela-

tion to mankind has been completed, written in a book and made available to the people of all nations with nothing more to be added, there is no further need for a separate people or nation to serve that purpose. But until that purpose was accomplished, the selection of Israel as a separated nation, the gift to them of the country of Palestine, together with the priesthood, the temple, the ritual, the sacrificial system, the Sabbath, the line of inspired prophets and the special laws that set them apart so effectively from the other people of the world, remained in effect. No element of that system could be ignored.

Since the Messiah has come and has fully performed his work of atonement, this special role assigned to the Jews has been fulfilled. Hence there remains no reason whatever for reviving or re-establishing any one or more of the elements of the old system. All of those elements belonged to the kindergarten stage of redemption, and on completion of that atonement at Calvary, all of those things passed away as a unit. What Paul termed the "dividing wall of hostility" between Jew and Gentile has been broken down, and it is never to be raised up again. Christ performed his work equally for men of all nationalities and races. It now makes no difference whether one be Jew, American, Japanese, German, Russian, white, black, red or yellow. He has the same right of approach to God through Christ, the same forgiveness of sins, the same hope of heaven.

That was the meaning of the supernatural rending of the curtain which separated the holy place from the holy of holies in the temple, symbolizing that the last sacrifice, which was Christ himself, had been offered and that God was leaving his temple, never to return. By that divine act the old order of ritual and incense, of the sacrificial blood of bulls and goats, of the temple and a human priesthood, and of the Jews as a separate people and Palestine as a separate land—all of that as a unit had fulfilled its purpose and was abolished forever.

In Matthew 24:30, in the final discourse of Jesus with his disciples, after telling them of the coming destruction of the temple and the hardships that the people would suffer, he made a strange statement: "Then will appear the sign of the Son of man in heaven." The Son of man would be in heaven, but the sign would be on the earth, namely, the destruction of the temple which would be the final sign that the Mosaic system, which centered in the temple, was finished, abolished, ended forever. What a terrible stumbling block the continued existence of the old Jewish temple would have been to the early church if it had been permitted to stand, pulling the people back to Judaism! What a stumbling block it would be even to the church today if it were still in existence!

We see no special mission in the future for the Jews, other than that they individually, like those of all other nationalities, be converted to Christianity as the church progresses throughout the world.

AN AMILLENNIAL RESPONSE
ANTHONY A. HOEKEMA

There is indeed a great deal in Ladd's essay with which I agree. I agree with him that the Old Testament must be interpreted in the light of the New Testament and that a totally and exclusively literal interpretation of Old Testament prophecy is not justified. I agree that the church is often spoken of in the New Testament as spiritual Israel and that the basic dispensationalist principle of an absolute distinction between Israel and the church, involving two distinct purposes of God and two distinct peoples of God, has no biblical warrant. I concur wholeheartedly with what is said about the present spiritual reign of Christ and about the present reality of the kingdom of God.

Our basic disagreement concerns the interpretation of Revelation 20:1-6. I was happy to note Ladd's admission that this passage is the only place in the Bible which speaks of a millennium (p. 32). On this point, too, we are in agreement. But now the all-important question is, What does this passage mean?

Looking at the matter first from a broad perspective, Ladd and I differ on the relation between Revelation 20:1-6 and 19:11-16. Ladd's position is, "The events of Revelation 20 follow the vision of the Second Coming of Christ, which is pictured in 19:11-16" (p. 33). I agree that Revelation 19:11-16 describes the Second Coming of Christ. But I do not agree that what is described in chapter 20 necessarily follows chronologically what is described in chapter 19, any more than what is described in chapter 12 (the birth of the man-child) follows chronologically what is described in the last verses of chapter 11 (the judging of the dead and the giving of rewards to the saints). The reasons why I believe that Revelation 20:1 takes us back to the beginning of the New Testament era are given in my essay, pages 156-60.

Concentrating now on Revelation 20:1-6, I must admit that Ladd's interpretation of these verses is one that makes good sense and that is consonant with the interpretation of the relation between chapters 19 and 20 which he has adopted. I have no difficulty in recognizing his exegesis of the passage as a valid option for evangelicals, and I appreciate the careful, scholarly and lucid way in which he sets forth his views.

But we do differ in our interpretation of the passage. I trust, however, that he and others who share his views will be willing to recognize that my interpretation arises not from a liberal approach to Scripture nor from a cavalier disregard of the text but from a different understanding of the words before us.

My disagreement concerns the following four matters. First, Ladd does not say much about the binding of Satan described in verses 1-3. He does not tell us exactly what he thinks this binding means nor precisely what he understands by "deceive the nations no more." He does not relate the binding of Satan spoken of here to passages in the Gospels which speak of such a binding as having already begun at the time of Christ's first coming (see pp. 161-64 of my essay). I have tried to show that the binding of Satan in Revelation 20:1-3 can be understood to mean that Satan cannot prevent the spread of the gospel during the present age, that he cannot gather Christ's enemies together to attack the church, and that this binding takes place during the entire era of the New Testament church (see pp. 161-63).

Second, Ladd renders the Greek word *ezēsan*, in both of its occurrences in this passage, by "came to life" (p. 35). This is, to be sure, a possible rendering. Another equally possible rendering, however, is to render the word as the American Standard Version does: "lived."

Third, Ladd interprets *ezēsan* in both instances as describing a bodily resurrection. I agree with him that the word must mean the same thing both times it is used and that it is irresponsible exegesis to assign one meaning to the first occurrence of the word and a different meaning to the second. However, I understand the word as it is used here to mean not regeneration but the transition from physical death to life in heaven with Christ during the time between death and the resurrection (pp. 170-71). Deceased believers participate in this life whereas deceased unbelievers do not (pp. 167-71).

Ladd understands *ezēsan* in verses 4 and 5 as meaning bodily resurrection in both instances. In support of this interpretation he points to two other passages in the book of Revelation where *ezēsan* has this meaning: 2:8 and 13:14. I agree with him on 2:8 but not on 13:14. The latter passage speaks of the beast "which was wounded by the sword and yet lived." Ladd comments that the wound was a "mortal wound" or a wound unto death, and that therefore "lived" here means raised from the dead (p. 37). But verse 3, to which reference is made, does not say that the beast died but rather that "one of its heads *seemed* to have a mortal wound, but its mortal wound was healed" (my emphasis). The Greek word *hōs* used here tells us that the beast was not killed but only seemed to have been killed. For this reason I believe that "lived" (*ezēsan*) in verse 14 cannot mean bodily resurrection.

There are, however, other uses of the verb *zao*, of which *ezēsan* is one form, in the book of Revelation which do not mean bodily resurrection. In 7:2 and 15:7, for example, the word is used to describe the fact that God lives forever; in these instances it says nothing about bodily resurrection. In 3:1 it is used to describe what we might call spiritual life: "you have the name of being alive, and you are dead." The reference to other uses of the verb *zao* in the book of Revelation, therefore, cannot be decisive in this matter.

I would rather adduce the parallel to Revelation 20:4 and 5 which we find in chapter 6:9-11. Here, according to the NIV, John saw "the souls of those who had been slain because of the word of God and the testimony they had maintained" (note the similarity of language to 20:4, "the souls of those who had been beheaded because of their testimony for Jesus and because of the word of God" [NIV]). These souls of deceased martyrs are apparently conscious and capable of being addressed; they are given white robes and are told to be at rest. The white robes and the resting suggest that they are enjoying a provisional kind of blessedness which looks forward to the final eschaton. This is precisely the situation of the souls described in chapter 20, who are said to reign with Christ while waiting for the resurrection of the body which has not yet occurred (see 20:11-13). Although the word *lived* (*ezēsan*) is not used in 6:9-11, the situation described in those verses is parallel to the situation described in 20:4.

My interpretation of the meaning of *ezēsan*, therefore, is not out of harmony with the rest of the book of Revelation. It is also not out of harmony with the rest of chapter 20 which predicts the resurrection of the body and the final judgment at the end of the chapter, after the description of the thousand-year reign. Though the resurrection which is described in verses 11-15 is commonly understood by premillennialists as the resurrection of the unbelieving dead only, there is no indication in these verses that the resurrection there depicted is limited to the unbelieving dead. To be sure, verse 15 says, "if any one's name was not found written in the book of life, he was thrown into the lake of fire." But is there any indication that none of those here said to have been raised from the dead were found written in the book of life?

Fourth, I agree that the rule of Christ is now mostly invisible (though not entirely so) and that we look forward to the total visible expression of this rule after Christ's return. But why limit this visible expression to a thousand-year period? Why should this visible expression of Christ's rule still have to occur, as Ladd says on page 39, "*in history*" (meaning, in "the world as we now know it," in distinction from the world to come)? Why, for example, should believers be raised from the dead to live on an earth which is not yet glorified and which is still groaning because of the presence of sin, rebellion and death (see Rom. 8:19-22)? Why should the glorified Christ have to come back to earth to rule over his enemies with a rod of iron and thus still have to endure opposition to his sovereignty? Was not this phase of his work completed during his state of humiliation? Is Christ not coming back in the fulness of his glory to usher in, not an interim period of qualified peace and blessing, but the final state of unqualified perfection?

II

DISPENSATIONAL PREMILLENNIALISM

DISPENSATIONAL PREMILLENNIALISM HERMAN A. HOYT

A world in turmoil yearns for a period in history when mankind can enjoy the benefits of the millennial kingdom as described in the Bible, a golden age of civilization. This millennial kingdom will be ushered in by a divine, supernatural and catastrophic manifestation from heaven at the Second Coming of Christ. It will be established on the earth when the conditions of life have reached the depths of great tribulation. The movement of events in our day suggests that the establishment of the kingdom is not far away.

But let us not imagine that all theologians agree on this point. In fact no area of predictive prophecy has escaped the differing opinions of students of Scripture. Just as various areas of Christianity disagree vigorously on the issues of the rapture of the church, the great tribulation and the eternal state, so also there is disagreement on the subject of the millennial kingdom.

My approach to this topic is often characterized as the premillennial approach from the dispensational angle. I prefer to regard this view as the ordered and progressive unfolding of this theme in the prophetic Scriptures. More properly, the millennial kingdom is one aspect of the larger theme of the Scriptures on the kingdom of God.

The Kingdom Declared by Scripture

Regardless of the particular eschatological persuasion of the theologian, if he is attempting to make a serious effort at expounding the Scriptures, he must unhesitatingly admit that the Bible presents a doctrine of the kingdom of God. The word *kingdom* itself appears more than four hundred and fifty times in the Bible. Approximately two hundred of these appearances set forth a divine, eschatological kingdom. But the teaching is in no sense confined to the word *kingdom*. The idea goes far beyond specific terminology and runs through the entire Bible. John Bright declares,

> For the concept of the Kingdom of God involves, in a real sense, the total message of the Bible. Not only does it loom large in the teachings of Jesus; it is to be found, in one form or another, through the length and breadth of the Bible. . . . Old Testament and New Testament thus stand together as the two acts of a single drama. Act I points to its conclusion in Act II, and without it the play is an incomplete, unsatisfying thing. But Act II must be read in the light of Act I, else its meaning will be missed. For the play is organically one. The Bible is one book. Had we to give that book a title, we might with justice call it "The Book of the Coming Kingdom of God."[1]

The issue of dominion is introduced in the opening chapter of the Bible. Immediately after creating man in the image of God the first command given to him concerns the exercise of sovereign control over creation (Gen. 1:26, 28). This theme unfolds in progressive wonder through the Bible until at last the throne of God is established on the earth (Rev. 22:1, 3) and the redeemed saints reign with Christ forever (Rev. 22:5).

Such Scriptures as the following mark the movement of thought through the Bible. They indicate that the purpose of God is to establish a kingdom on the earth. At Sinai the Lord organized Israel into a kingdom of priests (Ex. 19:5-6) and Moses the mediator of his word to the people (Ex. 7:1; Acts 7:35). A prophet like Moses was promised for the future to whom all the people would give submission (Deut. 18:15-18; Acts 3:19-23). David was anointed king over Israel and his kingdom was to last forever (2 Sam. 7:12-16), and this was perpetuated through Solomon (1 Chron. 28:5, 7). The prophet Isaiah announced the coming of a king and a kingdom of which there would be no end (Is. 9:6-7). Daniel later declared that the God of heaven will set up this kingdom, and it shall never be destroyed (Dan. 2:44). One like the son of man shall sit upon the throne of this kingdom and all peoples, nations and languages shall serve him (Dan. 7:13-14, 27). The angel sent to Mary informed her that God would give to her son the throne of his father David, and his reign over the house of Jacob would be forever (Lk. 1:32-33). During his postresurrection ministry, Christ taught the disciples the things pertaining to this kingdom and aroused in them the question of its restoration to Israel (Acts 1:3, 6). Paul encouraged the saints to live in anticipation of the appearing of the King and his kingdom (2 Tim. 4:1). And in the final book of the Bible, at the sounding of the seventh trumpet, it is declared that this long awaited kingdom has at last "become the kingdom of our Lord, and of his Christ: and he shall reign for ever and ever" (Rev. 11:15, ASV).

The Principle for Interpreting Scripture
The message of the Bible was directed to the people of God in both the Old Testament and New Testament periods. Moses made this fact clear in his closing addresses to the people of Israel on the plains of Moab. "The secret things belong to the

LORD our God; but the things that are revealed belong to us
and to our children for ever, that we may do all the words of
this law" (Deut. 29:29). Through centuries God sent prophets
to the nation of Israel to reveal his will (Mt. 23:37). Over and
over again in the New Testament it is clearly indicated that its
message was intended for the saints of the church (Lk. 1:3-4;
Jn. 20:30-31; Acts 1:1; Rom. 1:7; Phil. 1:1).

This message was sent to the people in order that certain
moral and spiritual benefits might be realized by them. The
Scriptures constituted a message and a method of making
them wise unto salvation (2 Tim. 3:15). It instructed them in
the word and will of God (Deut. 29:29; 2 Tim. 3:16-17). It
provided words of encouragement and comfort (Rom. 15:4).
It served to warn them of the perils in the way (1 Cor. 10:11).
And beyond all this, it gave them hope in the midst of the
darkness and dread of this world (Rom. 15:4).

For this reason the message had to be given in a simple,
straightforward and clear way (1 Cor. 2:1-5) if it was to reach
the minds of the people and accomplish what God intended.
In the good providence of God even the language of the Bible
is the common language of the people to whom it was originally sent. The Old Testament is written in the Hebrew that was
familiar to the people, and the language of the New Testament was the vernacular of those from one end of the Roman
Empire to the other. This made the message accessible to the
rank and file who belonged to God. No special class, such as
prophets, teachers, theologians or ecclesiastics, stood between
the people and this message.

All this argues for a principle of interpretation that brings
the meaning of the Bible within the grasp of the rank and file
of the people of God. This principle clearly stated is that of
taking the Scriptures in their literal and normal sense, understanding that this applies to the entire Bible. This means that
the historical content of the Bible is to be taken literally; the

doctrinal material is also to be interpreted in this way; the moral and spiritual information likewise follows this pattern; and the prophetic material is also to be understood in this way. This does not mean that there is not figurative language used in the Bible. But it does mean that where such language is employed, it is an application of the literal method to interpret the passage in that way. Any other method of interpretation partially, if not completely, robs God's people of the message which was intended for them.

The literal method of approach to the teaching of the premillennial, dispensational doctrine of the kingdom is absolutely basic. Both friends and enemies of this doctrine freely admit that this is foundational to the doctrine. Walvoord, a clear exponent of premillennialism, asserts,

Premillennialism is founded principally on interpretation of the Old Testament. If interpreted literally, the Old Testament gives a clear picture of the prophetic expectation of Israel. They confidently anticipated the coming of a Savior and Deliverer, a Messiah who would be Prophet, Priest, and King. They expected that He would deliver them from their enemies and usher in a kingdom of righteousness, peace, and prosperity upon a redeemed earth. . . . The premillennial interpretation offers the only literal fulfillment for the hundreds of verses of prophetic testimony.[2]

Determined foes of this method of interpretation are just as clear in their admissions of the importance of the literal approach to the Scriptures to establish the doctrine of premillennialism. Allis unequivocally admits, "The Old Testament prophecies if literally interpreted cannot be regarded as having been fulfilled or as being capable of fulfillment in this present age."[3] Floyd Hamilton, equally opposed to premillennialism, regretfully concedes the same point:

Now we must frankly admit that a literal interpretation of the Old Testament prophecies gives us just such a picture of an earthly reign of the Messiah as the premillennialist pictures. That was the kind of a Messianic kingdom that the Jews of the time of Christ were looking for, on the basis of a literal interpretation of the Old Testament.[4]

Where premillennialism prevails it will be observed that it is not only founded on the literal interpretation of the Scriptures, but that from this point on it proceeds to erect an entire system of theology that incorporates the entire Bible. Beginning with the infallibility of the Scriptures, it reaches out and touches every facet of Christian doctrine. In fact it is the unifying principle that enables the believer to see every aspect of the Christian faith in its proper relation to the whole. Contrary to the charges that have been leveled against premillennialism, it is not based upon a few isolated texts nor even on an arbitrary selection of texts. It is a system of theology comprising the Bible, confronting the problems of the Bible, confining itself to the Bible and commending hope to a world miserably failing and seized with fear.

Above all, premillennialism provides a philosophy of history that is the best and brightest of all philosophies. It takes into consideration every aspect of reality. It gives consideration to the life that now is and that which is to come (1 Tim. 4:8). It is concerned with the natural and also the spiritual (1 Cor. 15:46). It recognizes the place of the earthly and also the heavenly (1 Cor. 15:48). It places a value on life in the present and on the earthly level as well as regarding life on the heavenly plane as worthwhile. It sees the importance of history (Rom. 15:4; 1 Cor. 10:11), and suggests that we can learn something reliable for application to the present and for expectation in the future.

Premillennialism points to the fact that God is progressively moving through history and directing the course of events to some good end. It is true that through sin humanity has failed. But in spite of that fact the movement of history is forward and upward, and will at last come to a grand consummation in the future under the power of God. We have failed because we turned our faces from God. But we succeed by the power of God in the conquering of disease, the prevention of some wars, the adding of years to the span of life, the elimination of some social and political ills, the conquering of space and the increase of productiveness of the soil. All this points to that day when within the context of the power and grace of God, and on the earthly level, there will be ushered in the golden age of all civilization.

This sort of philosophy makes sense. It gives meaning to human effort. It provides an atmosphere of optimism to history. It provides the incentive for the exercise of all the aspirations and efforts of mankind to strive for that which is better, realizing that all the true values of life will be preserved and will reach their complete fulfillment in that coming kingdom of our Lord and Savior Jesus Christ.[5]

Interpretations of the Kingdom

Because theologians have approached the subject of the kingdom with differing principles of interpretation, a variety of interpretations have arisen. A survey of nine of these views will be helpful in reaching the biblical view.[6]

1. Before Christ, there were Jews who believed that this kingdom was limited to Israel. Even the apostles were of this mind. This led them to raise the question about the restoration of the kingdom to Israel (Acts 1:6).

2. The phrase "the kingdom of heaven" has caused some to identify the kingdom with heaven, insisting that it concerns the reign of God in heaven. A passage like Matthew 19:23-24 is explained to mean going to heaven now, while Matthew 25:34 refers to the future.

3. By spiritualizing Scripture the church has been understood to be the totality of the kingdom. Passages such as Colos-

sians 1:13 have been used to support this view. Roman Catholicism interpreted the visible hierarchy to be the kingdom
while Reformation theologians pointed to the invisible
church.

4. Some theologians were so dominated by the spiritualization principle that they interpreted the rule of God in the
heart to be the kingdom. Inasmuch as the new birth results
in the impartation of new life, Luke 17:20-21 was cited in
proof of this view.

5. To escape the sheer materialistic and carnal explanation
of the kingdom, some men gravitated toward high morality
and spiritual purpose, and found in Romans 14:17 a text that
in their estimation supported this view of the kingdom.

6. Within recent years social organization and overall improvement of mankind offered a welcome explanation of a
present kingdom as over against a future eschatological kingdom. The whole ecumenical movement is conditioned by this
pattern of reasoning.

7. Some men have dared to charge the Bible writers, and
even the Lord Jesus Christ, with delusions of grandeur. They
took the text of the Bible literally but asserted that it was absolutely wrong, thus disposing of the whole eschatological system.

8. Barth and Brunner brought to the attention of the
Christian public a most fantastic view of the kingdom. They
lifted it out of the cycle of time-space events of history and
placed it in the realm of eternity which belongs alone to God.

9. The biblical view, taking the Scriptures at face value, is
a kingdom established on the earth at the Second Coming of
Christ. This was the view of the early church, a view which
persisted for the first two and one-half centuries. Not until
the time of Augustine did any opposing view gain a propo-
nent of sufficient stature to turn men aside from premillennialism.

The Biblical Interpretation of the Kingdom

An examination of the above reveals that there is widespread disagreement among theologians as to the nature of the kingdom. Much of this disagreement undoubtedly arises from narrow and one-sided opinions. Limited perspective in the study of the kingdom has produced this situation. Some have not fully comprehended what Daniel declared in his prophecy concerning "the greatness of the kingdom" (Dan. 7:27). In an effort to reduce the subject of the kingdom to a single principle, they have ignored the infinite variety in favor of a barren unity.

These facts make it clear that any approach to the biblical phrase "kingdom of God" must be pursued with a biblical pattern of interpretation if the result is to be an authoritative meaning, as assigned to it in the Word of God. An inductive study of the biblical material alone will yield positive results. The true conception of the kingdom dare not rest on any single text or passage. All the biblical material must be surveyed, and this examination must be made in relation to the movement of history and the progress of divine revelation following the method of biblical theology.

In the opening pages of his classic work, *The Greatness of the Kingdom*, McClain gives a tentative definition of the concept of a *kingdom*:

A general survey of the Biblical material indicates that the concept of a "kingdom" envisages a total situation containing at least three essential elements: first, a ruler with adequate authority and power; second, a realm of subjects to be ruled; and third, the actual exercise of the function of rulership.[7]

The above explanation makes it clear that there can be no kingdom without all three elements existing in a proper relationship to one another. Even though it is true that the most important element is the ruler with authority, apart from

realm or rulership there can be no kingdom in the fundamental sense. With respect to the kingdom of God then, it may
be broadly defined as the rule of God over his creatures.

A perusal of the passages on the kingdom reveals some
rather important distinctions. Many passages present the
kingdom as something that has *always existed* (Ps. 10:16), yet
other texts suggest that the kingdom is to have a *definite beginning* (Dan. 2:44). Some passages picture the kingdom as *universal* in scope (Ps. 103:19), but still others set forth the kingdom as a *local* rule on the earth (Is. 24:23). In some passages
God is depicted as *ruling directly* (Ps. 59:13) while in others he
rules through a mediator (Ps. 2:4-6). Many texts present the kingdom as something that is wholly *future* (Zech. 14:9), and in
others it is described as a *present reality* (Ps. 29:10). In many
places the kingdom is described as the *unconditional* rule of
God over his creatures (Dan. 4:34-35), but elsewhere this rule
is based upon a *covenant* negotiated by God with men (Ps. 89:
27-29).

Many have attempted to reconcile these conflicting distinctions concerning the kingdom, some concluding one or
more of the following: there is one kingdom with two aspects;
there are two kingdoms, one of power and another of grace;
God's rule is universal sovereignty on the one hand and a
theocratic rule on the other; God is King now but his kingship
is still future; there is a present and victorious reality but a
future rule far more victorious; there is a kingdom of Christ
and a kingdom of God; there is a kingdom of God and a kingdom of heaven; or there is a kingdom on earth and a kingdom
over the earth.

The most reasonable explanation recognizes the existence
of two kingdoms, but care must be exercised to guard against
the false notion that these kingdoms are wholly distinct from
one another. They constitute two aspects or phases of the one
rule of God over his creatures. Two terms therefore com-

mend themselves to the premillennialist as best describing these aspects of God's rule. The first is *universal*, describing the extent of God's rule. The second is *mediatorial*, describing the method of God's rule. In each case it is the quality or nature of God's rule that identifies it.

Before proceeding to a discussion of the mediatorial kingdom, which is the proper area of discussion here, it seems wise to list a series of distinctions differentiating the universal kingdom from the mediatorial kingdom. The universal kingdom is everlasting (Ps. 145:13). It encompasses all creation (1 Chron. 29:12). The rule is almost wholly providential, that is, through second causes (Ex. 14:21; Ps. 29:3; Is. 10:5-15). There are times when rule is ministered by supernatural means such as miraculous events (Ex. 11:9; Deut. 4:34-35; Dan. 6:27). The universal kingdom operates, irrespective of the attitudes of the subjects (Ps. 103:20; Dan. 4:35; Acts 3:17-18; 1 John 3:4, 8, ASV). The universal kingdom is always mediated through the eternal Son (Col. 1:17, ASV marg.; Heb. 1:2). The universal kingdom is not specifically like the kingdom for which Christ urges his disciples to pray (Mt. 6:10). The universal kingdom is always present while the mediatorial kingdom is a promise for the future. When at last the purpose of God is accomplished in the mediatorial kingdom, and every enemy is at last brought into subjection to the Son (1 Cor. 15:24-28), then the mediatorial kingdom will be merged with the universal kingdom and there will be one throne (Rev. 22:3).

The discussion up to this point should make it clear that there are three areas correctly referred to as the kingdom of God. There is first of all the universal kingdom of God (Ps. 103:19). Within this larger area there is the more limited sphere known as the mediatorial kingdom (Dan. 2:44). Within the area of the mediatorial kingdom there is an even more restricted area, namely, the church which partakes of certain characteristics of the universal kingdom and the mediatorial kingdom. So it is quite proper for Paul to refer to a saint being translated into the kingdom of Christ (Col. 1:13). The mediatorial kingdom belongs to members of the church in the sense that as the bride of Christ and the queen, she will rule and reign with Christ in this kingdom (Heb. 12:28; Rev. 3:21).

The History of the Mediatorial Kingdom

From this point on the discussion will be confined to the biblical area of the mediatorial kingdom. Keep in mind that by the kingdom of God we mean the rule of God over his creation. Inasmuch as the mediatorial kingdom is the first phase in the realization of the everlasting or universal kingdom, much that describes the mediatorial kingdom will also be true of the universal kingdom.

Since we have chosen to use the word *mediatorial* as referring to this kingdom, it should be recognized that this limits the word kingdom to a particular concept. This means that God exercises control over this kingdom through a divinely chosen representative who speaks and acts for God with the people on the one hand and on the other represents the people to God. It is clear that this kingdom has a special relation to the human race on the earth and that the mediator is always a member of the human race. Even though the word mediator does not appear at all in the Old Testament, there is a word very similar, the word *daysman* or *umpire* (Job 9:33, KJV, ASV). However, the New Testament does use a word that means mediator (*mesites*), and it appears six times (Gal. 3:19-20; 1 Tim. 2:5; Heb. 8:6; 9:15; 12:24). The functions of the mediator are threefold—that of prophet, priest and king.

In the progressive unfolding of revelation on the mediatorial kingdom, the length of this kingdom is not revealed until the final book of the Bible. Six times in the first seven verses of Revelation 20, it is declared that this kingdom is a thousand years in length. In the Latin translation the word *millennium* renders the Greek word for a thousand, and that explains the term as used for this kingdom.

The preparation for the inauguration of the mediatorial kingdom in history began at creation. God created man in his own image, which included the potentialities for dominion, and then actually commanded him to exercise this divinely derived function (Gen. 1:26-28). This was to extend to "all the earth," including mankind. Humanity did not hesitate to exercise this function but failed in that we refused to recognize that it was derived (Rom. 5:12, 19; 1 Tim. 2:14). This introduced chaos and disorder into the earthly scene (Gen. 4: 19-24) which eventually brought abandonment by God (Gen. 6:3) and universal catastrophe (Gen. 6:1-13). Human government failed (Gen. 9:5-6) and required the judgment of the confusion of tongues to halt the wicked world government (Gen. 11:1-9).

At this point God turned in a new direction to accomplish his will. He sought to rule his people through the mediation of patriarchs. He called Abraham out of Ur of the Chaldees (Gen. 12:1-3), and through this man were to come kings (Gen. 17:6) who would serve in the capacity of genuine mediators, exercising absolute authority (Gen. 14:14; 21:9-21; 22:1-19). Beginning with Abraham, in the line of succession there follows Isaac, Jacob, Joseph, Moses, Joshua, the judges, Samuel and then the kings discharging the responsibility of mediatorial control.

In the more formal sense the mediatorial kingdom had its origin in Moses at the Exodus from Egypt, at Mount Sinai and during the sojourn in the wilderness. "By signs, by wonders, . . . and by great terrors" (Deut. 4:34) the people were compelled to believe in a supernatural God ruling through his appointed ruler Moses. In these events there came "the birth of Israel as a nation."[8] Though Moses is not referred to as king, he performed regal functions (Acts 7:35). As mediator he represented God to the people (Ex. 4:16; 7:1), and the people to God (Deut. 9:24-29). In this way Moses became the type of the coming perfect mediator, Christ (Deut. 18:15).

The magnificence of this mediatorial kingdom in history reaches its fullness during the reign of Saul, David and Solomon. This monarchical form was foreseen in prophecy (Gen. 17:5-7; 35:9-11), and certain cautions were laid down (Deut. 17:14-17). Spiritual deterioration during the period of the judges led to the choice of a king (Judg. 8:22-23; 1 Sam. 8:1-9, 19-22). But God chose the king (1 Sam. 10:17-24; 12:1-25). During this entire period from Moses to Solomon the presence of the Shekinah glory indicated God's approval on the mediatorial regency (Ex. 40:34; 2 Chron. 7:1; Neh. 9:19).

From Rehoboam on, there was a gradual decline in the mediatorial function so that the rule of God became more indirect. At this point prophets entered the scene. This was God's way of getting his message to the people despite the failure of the kings. This decline was foreseen in every stage of its deterioration (1 Sam. 8:7-20). Prophets diagnosed the spiritual conditions in Israel (Is. 1:3-6) and called for a return to the law (Is. 8:20) in view of approaching judgment (Amos 5:18-24). But the inviolability of the kingdom covenant (Jer. 33:17-21) led the prophets to promise a future and an ideal kingdom (Zech. 14:7-9).

But apostasy and degeneration in Israel inevitably brought the disapproval of the Lord and his departure. The presence of the Shekinah glory from Sinai on had been the symbol of God's presence among his people. But the desperate rebellion and descent into sin by the time of Ezekiel reached the crucial point. So God gave a vision to Ezekiel of the reluctance and gradual departure of the glory from Israel (Ezek. 8:3-4; 9:3; 10:4, 18; 11:23; see also 8:7-17). Since the people had forsaken God, God now forsook the nation. Though there were two later temples after the destruction of Solomon's temple by Nebuchadnezzar, there was no glory. In the historical sense the mediatorial kingdom had been interrupted. But in the good providence of God, divine promise was given to Israel for the future (Ezek. 11:16; 39:21-29; 43:1-7; Zech. 14:1-4).

The explanation for the failure of the mediatorial kingdom in history must be traced to three things. Spiritually, the majority of the people were not in sympathy with the Lord nor in harmony with his laws. Intellectually, the people were convinced that in order to succeed, Israel must conform to the nations round about (1 Sam. 8:5, 20). Moreover, politically, the rulers were filled with imperfections.

The promise for the future will remedy these weaknesses. The vast majority of the people will have experienced the new birth (Ezek. 11:17-20) and will therefore be in harmony with the King and his laws (Ps. 110:1-3). Imperfect kings will be supplanted by a perfect mediatorial King, the Lord Jesus Christ (Is. 42:1-4) who is fully subject to God, separated from the empty sensationalism of the world, discharging a saving ministry toward his subjects and able to carry his program through to complete success.

Since 600 B.C. many efforts have been made to revive the ancient Jewish state, but without success. Even the present state of Israel is not to be construed as the incipient stage of the mediatorial kingdom, though it may be a token of what lies ahead. The final and permanent state of Israel is inseparably bound up with the mediatorial kingdom and awaits the coming of the Lord Jesus Christ. The mediatorial kingdom will be restored (Acts 1:6), and prophecy declares that it is a certain event for the future (Hos. 3:4-5).

The Kingdom in Prophecy

Actual historic situations provided the occasion for predictive prophecy concerning the mediatorial kingdom. Starting with an event or person in the near future, the prophet moved to some event or person in the more remote future of Israel and the mediatorial kingdom. When the near event arrived it became the earnest and divine foreshadowing of the far and final event (Is. 13:17—14:4; see 14:5-6).

Old Testament prophecy begins with a few scattered and somewhat obscure references in the books of Moses. For the most part this centers on the mediatorial King. He will be the seed of the woman (Gen. 3:15), dwelling in the tents of Shem (Gen. 9:27), coming through Abraham (Gen. 12:1-4), a lawgiver from Judah (Gen. 49:10), a star out of Jacob (Num. 24:17) and a prophet like Moses (Deut. 18:15). During the period of the historical kingdom, prominent use is made of double reference in kingdom prophecy (2 Sam. 7:1-16; 1 Chron. 17:1-14). David is assured that his house, kingdom and throne will be established forever (1 Chron. 17:1-4; 2 Sam. 7:14). This must have its complete fulfillment in Christ who is his seed (Luke 1:31-33). Solomon is also assured of the same thing (1 Chron. 22:6-10). As Israel declines, Old Testament prophecy increases, the record of which is to be found in all the major and minor prophets. In this area of predictive prophecy is to be found a clear description of the coming kingdom.

It will be a *literal* kingdom in every sense of that word. This kingdom is not an abstract ideal toward which men are striving but will never attain. It will be as real as any kingdom on the face of the earth, as real as the historical kingdom in Israel. The actual place of its central location will be Jerusalem and vicinity (Obad. 12-21). A real King will sit on a material throne (Is. 33:17). Nations of mankind will participate in its ministry of welfare and deliverance (Is. 52:10). The wicked kingdoms of this world will be brought to a sudden and catastrophic end at the coming of Christ, and his kingdom will supplant them (Dan. 2:31-45). This kingdom will be a revival and continuation of the historical Davidic kingdom (Amos 9:11; see Acts 15:16-18). A faithful and regenerated remnant of Israel will be restored and made the nucleus of this kingdom, and thus the covenant with David will be fulfilled (Mic. 4:7-8; Jer. 33: 15-22; Ps. 89:3-4, 34-37). Jerusalem will become the capital city of the great King, from which he will govern the world (Is. 2:3; 24:23).

The *manifestation* of the mediatorial kingdom is also literal. It is something that is a part of the progressive unfolding of events in a time sequence. Some prophets envisioned it as near at hand and used phrases like "a little while" (Hag. 2:6-9) and "a very little while" (Is. 29:17-20). At other times prophets referred to this event as farther removed into the future, as taking place in the "latter days" (Is. 2:2, ASV). Hosea declares that Israel "shall dwell many days" before this event occurs (Hos. 3:4-5). Ultimately, these time measurements must be evaluated from God's viewpoint (2 Pet. 3:8-10). But when the kingdom is established it will be preceded by a series of world-wide judgments felt in the whole fabric of nature: sun, moon, stars, earthquake, flood, fire, famine and pestilence, all affecting the nations of mankind (Is. 24; Joel 2:30-31; 3:9-15). All this will be the prelude to the manifestation of God and his glory (Is. 35:4; 40:5, 9-10). All this means that the establishment of the kingdom will not be a long, drawn out process, but will be sudden, catastrophic, supernatural, in the realm of sense experience, so that all mankind will know that God is interrupting the course of human history and introducing something divine into the natural order (Is. 40:5; Ezek. 20: 33-38; Dan. 2:34, 44; Joel 3:1-2; Amos 9:9-10; Mal. 3:1-6; Mt. 25:31-46).

Central to the description of the coming kingdom is the *King*, a literal, divine-human person. A glory gathers about him to which no amount of space can do justice. His names and titles make it perfectly clear that he is both human and divine. He is set forth as "a man" (Is. 32:1-2, AV), "a shoot from the stump of Jesse" (Is. 11:1) and as the "son of man" (Dan. 7:13). On the other hand he is pointed to as "the LORD" (Ps. 2:7), "your God" (Is. 40:9-10), the "mighty God" (Is. 9:6). All the necessary qualifications for successful reign are present in him: a seven-fold plenitude of power (Is. 11:2), a perfect exercise of power in procedure (Is. 11:3-4) and a perfection of character such as righteousness and faithfulness (Is. 11:5). But there is a mystery about this person. In the course of his career, he is cut off (Dan. 9:26, ASV). The prophet recognizes something of the mystery of this servant, his sorrows, suffering submission, satisfaction (Is. 52:13—53:12). The sufferings and glory present in this one person confused the prophets, baffled men and mystified the apostles (1 Pet. 1: 10-12).

The *form of government* in the mediatorial kingdom is monarchical. This, too, is literal in meaning. The Bible says that "the government will be upon his shoulder" (Is. 9:6). While it is true that his right to the throne on the human side must be traced to the fact that he is the son of David, still the Bible makes it clear that the King receives and holds authority by divine grant. "To him was given dominion and glory and kingdom" (Dan. 7:14). The Father declares, "I have set my king on Zion, my holy hill" (Ps. 2:6). At his ascension Christ returned to heaven "to receive a kingdom and then return" (Lk. 19:12). All the functions of government will be vested in him: legislative, judicial, executive (Is. 33:17-24). This does not mean that he will perform every function personally, but it does mean that final authority rests with him, and he delegates and directs their performance. There will be a perfect blending of severity and tenderness. He will rule the nations with a rod of iron (Ps. 2:7-9, 12), and "he will gather the lambs in his arms, he will carry them in his bosom, and gently lead those that are with young" (Is. 40:11). "With righteousness he shall judge the poor, and decide with equity for the meek of the earth; and he shall smite the earth with the rod of his mouth, and with the breath of his lips he shall slay the wicked" (Is. 11:4). As a result of these supernatural qualities in full operation, "Of the increase of his government and peace there will be no end, upon the throne of David, and over his kingdom, to establish it, and to uphold it with justice and with righteousness from this time forth and for evermore" (Is. 9:7). As never before and at last, the golden age of civilization will be experienced on the earth.

The *external organization* of the mediatorial kingdom is an amazing phenomenon. No political structure has ever been devised like this one. In the place of supremacy, "a king will reign in righteousness" (Is. 32:1). "The LORD will become king over all the earth; on that day the LORD will be one and his name one" (Zech. 14:9). To a spiritual nobility the multiplied responsibilities of government will be delegated. This group is made up of three companies of resurrected saints: the church (1 Cor. 6:2; Rev. 3:21; 20:6), the Old Testament saints (Ezek. 37:24-25; Dan. 7:18, 22, 27), and the tribulation martyrs (Rev. 20:4). The redeemed living nation of Israel, regenerated and regathered to the land, will be head over all the nations of earth (Deut. 28:1, 13; Is. 41:8-16). Having graven that nation upon the palms of his hands, God cannot forget them (Is. 49:15-16). So he exalts them above the Gentile nations (Is. 60:1-3, 12). On the lowest level there are the saved, living, Gentile nations. They are organized as nations with kings or ruling monarchs, and possessing all the other subsidiary divisions belonging to good systems of government. These are the sheep of Matthew 25:34. Two nations are named in particular: Assyria and Egypt (Is. 19:23-25). They will worship the same Lord (Mic. 4:2) and make yearly pilgrimages to the city of the great King (Zech. 8:18-23; 14:16-19), and they will be owned by the Lord as "nations that are called by my name" (Amos 9:12, ASV).

Every aspect of a real kingdom will characterize the *essential nature* of the mediatorial kingdom. Not only will this kingdom be marked by universal change in the structure and operation of society, but the sweeping nature of this change, and the richness and greatness of the kingdom, may be set forth in the following six considerations gleaned from the prophetic Scriptures.

Basically, the kingdom will be *spiritual in nature*. This does not mean that it etherealizes. But it does mean that it belongs to and is governed by the Spirit of God. It possesses every tangible and material quality of a real kingdom, and these under the control and direction of the Holy Spirit. Forgiveness, direct knowledge of God (Jer. 31:34), righteousness (Jer. 23:5-6), spiritual cleansing (Ezek. 36:24-26) and regeneration (Ezek. 36:26-28) will all be present.

The fruit of spiritual control will be manifest in *ethical conduct*. A system of moral values will be operative during this period (Is. 40:4). The objective standard of the law will be the rule of measure (Mal. 4:4). This law will go forth from Jerusalem to the wide earth (Is. 2:3). And all questions of right and wrong will be settled within the context of this absolute standard (Is. 8:20). The moral worth of individuals will be given accurate and truthful appraisal (Is. 32:5). Retribution for wrong doing will be swift, unerring and inescapable (Is. 11:3-4; Mal. 3:1-5).

In this kingdom there will be a restoration of perfect *social relations*. War will be completely eliminated as a method of solving international disputes (Is. 2:4). Even the arts and industries devoted to war will be removed from the economy. The material, money and time previously used for warmaking will be turned to constructive enterprises. Every positive effort will be used to make the fruits of the soil and the genius of mankind available for everyone (Is. 65:21-22).

The curse will in large part be lifted so that it will result in a *physical transformation.* There will be geological changes (Zech. 14:3-4), climatic changes (Is. 32:15-16; 35:7), increased fertility of the soil (Is. 35:1-2; Amos 9:13), changes in animal nature (Is. 11:6-9; 65:25), healing for physical ills (Is. 33:24; 35:5-6), restoration of long life (Is. 65:20, 22), and the elimination of physical hazards (Is. 65:23; Ezek. 34:23-31).

Political changes will likewise characterize this kingdom. Jerusalem will be the city for the arbitration of national disputes, and the central authority will be sovereign and inflexible (Is. 24:4; Mic. 4:3). National security will be one of the benefits for all the nations (Is. 32:18; Mic. 4:4). Israel will be restored permanently to her land (Amos 9:14-15), resulting in the re-establishment and unification of the Jewish state (Ezek. 37), and a place of pre-eminence among the nations (Is. 60:10-14).

Religious purification will be seen as the ruler of this kingdom will follow the Melchizedekian pattern of being both king and priest (Ps. 110). He will be the one object of worship by all nations (Is. 66:23), and every nation will be under compulsion to avail itself of this privilege (Zech. 14:16-19). A central sanctuary will be established in Jerusalem for the use of the people of all nations (Ezek. 37:27-28), and the Shekinah glory will again take up its rightful place in the temple (Ezek. 43: 1-7). The original intention of God for Israel will be accomplished in this people becoming the leaders and teachers of religious truth (Is. 61:6).

These six aspects of the kingdom bring into bold relief something of its greatness. It is a view which is complete and satisfying, reconciling all legitimate viewpoints. Its dimensions are amazing. The land area is worldwide (Zech. 14:9). All nations come within its control (Ps. 72:8-11). All the essential elements contributing to human life are present (Zech. 14:20-21). Of its increase (the number one problem of kingdoms today) there will be no end (Is. 9:7). Its duration is eternal. The first phase is for a thousand years (Rev. 20:4-6). Then it will be merged with the eternal state and will go on forever (Ps. 45:6; Dan. 7:13-14; Mic. 4:7; 1 Cor. 15:24-28; Rev. 22:1-5).

The Kingdom in the Gospels

There is a mystery about the mediatorial kingdom as set forth in the Gospels which has produced a variety of interpretations. Amillennialists center their attention upon the spiritual elements, bypassing the social and political, and call it the New Testament kingdom. Liberals argue that Christ intended to establish a Christian social order resulting in the social improvement of mankind. The critical school insists that Christ accommodated himself to the idealism of the Old Testament prophets. The biblical view is to take the teaching of Christ at face value and realize that Christ was presenting the same kingdom as taught in the Old Testament.

Many formal announcements are to be found in the Gospels concerning this kingdom. It was heralded by an angel (Lk. 1:30-33), anticipated by the Magi (Mt. 2:1-2), announced by John the Baptist (Mt. 3:1-2) and preached by Christ (Mt. 4:17, 23), the twelve apostles (Mt. 10:5-7) and the seventy disciples (Lk. 10:11). Certain expressions mark the nearness of this kingdom. Christ is set forth as its source of power (Lk. 11:20). This is explained by the fact that the King was standing in their midst (Lk. 17:21, ASV marg.). The kingdom had drawn near for the King was present (Mk. 1:15; Lk. 10:9). It was quite correct to refer to this kingdom as the "kingdom of heaven" (heaven representing the one who dwells in heaven) and the "kingdom of God" (God designating the one who rules)—see Matthew 4:17 and Mark 1:15. The two expressions are therefore interchangeable (Mt. 19:23-24).

A careful study points up the fact that the kingdom of the

Gospels is identified with the mediatorial kingdom of Old Testament prophecy. The very name, "kingdom of heaven," was derived from the prophecies of Daniel (2:44; 7:13-14), and its ruler, the "son of man," comes from the same source. This explains why Christ constantly appealed to the Old Testament prophets in support of his message concerning the kingdom (Lk. 4:18-19—see Is. 61:1-2; Lk. 7:27—see Mal. 3:1; Lk. 20:41-44—see Ps. 110:1).

The Gospels always associate the kingdom declared by Christ with that kingdom of Old Testament prophecy. Its throne belongs to David (Lk. 1:30-33). Its ruler is the one proclaimed by Isaiah (Mt. 3:3—see Is. 40:3). Its light is Christ, the light Isaiah announced (Mt. 4:12-17—see Is. 9:1-2). At no point does Christ ever intimate that his conception of the kingdom is any different from that in Old Testament prophecy. After all, he came to fulfill the law and the prophets (Mt. 5:17-18). Literal fulfillment attended the events of his appearance on the earth. He was born in Bethlehem (Lk. 2:1-6—see Mic. 5:2-5), and he rode into Jerusalem on an ass (Mt. 2:1-5—see Zech. 9:9-10).

In many ways the message and ministry of Christ exhibit the various aspects of the kingdom as set forth in Old Testament prophecy. The spiritual becomes a condition for entrance (Jn. 3:3-5). The highest ethical standards are outlined and emphasized (Mt. 5:19-21, 27). Social results will be displayed by the subjects of the kingdom (Mt. 13:41-43; Lk. 6:20-21). Cleansing of the temple demonstrates religious purification (Mk. 11:15-17). Political reorganization is pointed out (Mt. 19:28; 25:31), and sweeping changes in the physical environment will take place (Mt. 9:35; 10:5-8).

In spite of the clear teaching of Christ, the King and his kingdom were rejected. At the time of the first announcement of the kingdom, Christ understood there was contingency. The offer of the kingdom was genuine, but so also was

the human contingency (Mt. 10:5-7; 15:24). "If you are willing to accept it, this is Elijah who is to come" (Mt. 11:13-15;
17:10-13). Knowing the outcome ahead of time, Christ proph-
esied this coming event (Jn. 2:19-22; 3:14-15). In confirmation of what he knew would happen, he met with opposition
from the very beginning of his public ministry. He was repu-
diated in Nazareth (Lk. 4:28-29). At the second passover they
sought to kill him (Jn. 5:18, 43). Even his popularity with the
common people varied from time to time. One day they
wanted to make him king, but the next they forsook him (Jn.
6:15, 60-66). The opposition grew steadily until it reached
crisis proportions. He was accused of blasphemy and being in
league with the devil (Mt. 9:3-6, 10-12, 34). His ministry on
the Sabbath aggravated the situation (Mt. 12:2, 14). Clearly
the nation of Israel had become confirmed in its sin (Mt.
12:24-45). This finally culminated in the death of Christ, the
rejection of the kingdom and its suspension for the present
(Mt. 12:38-40). Having rejected the King, the nation of Israel
rejected the kingdom Christ came to establish.

Realizing that the rejection of himself and his kingdom
was inevitable, Christ sought to prepare his own apostles for
this event. In a series of parables he charts the "mystery" form
of the kingdom through the period of Israel's rejection.
There will be a sowing of seed in anticipation of a future realization of the kingdom (Mt. 13:3-9). This will result in a myste-
rious growth (Mk. 4:26-30). The growth will be mixed (Mt. 13:
24-30), and it will be unusual (Mt. 13:31-32). Doctrinal error
will infiltrate the sphere of biblical profession and will spread
through the entire area (Mt. 13:33). A precious remnant of
Israel will remain in the field for redemption (Mt. 13:44), and
a pearl of great price, the church, also in the field will be redeemed (Mt. 13:45-46). In the end of the age there will be a
separation of the bad from the good (Mt. 13:47-50).

At this time Christ reveals plans for turning in another

direction to accomplish his purpose during the rejection of the kingdom. He is going to build the church, a new society of believers (Mt. 16:13-20). He also begins to instruct his disciples more clearly concerning the necessity of his death and resurrection (Mt. 16:21; 17:22-23; 20:17-22, 28; 21:33-42). But he also assures them that he will return in glory to establish his kingdom. In the transfiguration he gives them a preview of its literal nature (Mt. 16:27—17:8; 2 Pet. 1:16-18) and promises them that they will share in this kingdom (Mt. 19: 27-28; Lk. 22:28-30).

No important element of instruction was omitted as Christ prepared his own for what was ahead. He made it clear that there would be delay in establishing the kingdom (Lk. 19: 11-27). Even though he knew what would happen, as King he made a bona fide offer of the kingdom according to prophecy (Lk. 19:29-44; Zech. 9:9-10). He then gave a prophetic discourse charting the course of events which will intervene before his return to establish the kingdom (Lk. 21:5-31). Then comes the night of betrayal followed by trials. During all this he never changed his claims but continued to urge those claims as the mediatorial King of Old Testament prophecy (Mt. 26:63-66; 27:11; Mk. 14:61-62; Jn. 18:33-39).

So completely was the kingdom identified with the King that a rejection of him meant the rejection of the kingdom. The Gospels give a sixfold explanation for the rejection.[9] From the first it was evident that the spiritual requirements for entrance to the kingdom were too high to be accepted (Mt. 5:20; 6:2, 5, 16). The refusal of Christ to set up a kingdom that was merely social and political in nature grew out of this (Lk. 12:13-14). The scathing denunciation of Christ directed at mere outward, ceremonial, traditional religion aroused the Jews (Lk. 11:37-41). The arraignment of the civil and religious leadership in Israel before the judgment bar of absolute truth constituted further reason for rejection (Mt. 23; Lk.

11:42—12:1). The amazing association of Christ with sinners in order to bring them to salvation could not be tolerated by the Jews (Lk. 15:1-2). Above all other reasons for condemnation were the exalted claims he made for himself and his conduct on the Sabbath (Jn. 5:16-18).

Christ and his kingdom experienced complete rejection by Israel. The entire nation was represented at the Passover (Lk. 23:13-35). Three classes of people made up the nation: the "rulers" or civil authorities (13), the "priests" or religious leadership (13), and the "people" or citizenry of the nation (35). Even though it appeared that the people were loyal to him almost to the end (Lk. 19:48—20:8, 19-26; 21:37—22:2), at last there came a change incited by the priests (Mk. 15:8-15). This demonstrated that the people were basically devoted to their leadership. They considered it the priests' right to speak with authority on matters of religion. Their hero disappointed them, for he did not come through with the social and material benefits that they had hoped to obtain (Jn. 6: 14-16, 66). So rulers, priests and people joined in totality as a nation to reject completely the King and his kingdom.

The Kingdom during the Present Age

The present age is to be regarded as a period of transition for the mediatorial kingdom. There was continued expectancy for its establishment (Acts 1:6), but believers were unable to harmonize this hope with the cross and the tomb (Lk. 24: 13-27, 44-45). It was the time element that mystified them (1 Pet. 1:10-12). However, at no point was the former teaching of Christ invalidated by the new directives given by the Lord (Acts 1:8; Mt. 28:16-20; Lk. 24:47-49).

New assurances were given to believers after the ascension of Christ as further confirmation of the teaching of Christ. Signs and wonders promised in Old Testament prophecy continued during the early period of the church. There was the

outpouring of the Spirit at Pentecost (Acts 2:1-4, 16-18), healing of the sick (Acts 3:1-10; 19:11-12—see Is. 35:1-10), physical wonders (Acts 4:31; 8:39; 16:26—see Joel 2:28-32), judgment upon sinners (Acts 5:1-11; 12:23; 13:11—see Ezek. 11:
13), miraculous visions (Acts 7:55; 9:3, 10; 11:5—see Joel 2:
28-32) and direct angelic ministry (Jn. 1:51; Acts 5:19; 10:3;
12:7; Heb. 1:6-7, 14).

Other offers of the kingdom also occurred during this
transitional period. At Pentecost Peter addressed the nation
(Acts 2:14-41) and pointed out the fact that the coming of the
Spirit was a fulfillment of prophecy (16-21) which certified
that Christ had been made both Lord and Christ (23-36). This
brought great conviction upon the people, and they were
urged to repent and turn to Christ. Three thousand respond-
ed (37-41). On a later occasion a miraculous healing provided
the platform. Peter again confronted the people with Christ
and his kingdom, and urged them to repent and be converted
that their "sins may be blotted out, that times of refreshing
may come from the presence of the Lord, and that he may
send the Christ appointed . . . Jesus" (Acts 3:19-20).

Following the pattern of the Gospels, there was growing
opposition among the Jews to the teaching concerning the
King and his kingdom. The Sadducees were definitely against
Christ and the supernatural (Acts 4:1-4). The Pharisees were
divided in their attitude toward the new sect (Acts 5:33-39).
Jewish riots were incited against the preaching of Christ (Acts
22:22-23; 23:10-12). At last the apostles were forced to turn
from the Jews to the Gentiles with their message of Christ and
his kingdom (Acts 13:43-48; 18:5-6; 19:8-9; 28:17-31). As the
tide of opposition grew the message concerning the kingdom
gradually receded from view, and the message concerning the
church came into prominence. The glory of the kingdom and
its prospect faded, and the church with a glory all its own became pre-eminent. But the message of the kingdom did not

entirely disappear. For God's purpose in this age was to form an aristocracy for the kingdom; the church was to be associated with Christ in ruling and reigning over that kingdom (1 Cor. 4:8; 6:2; Heb. 12:28).

In a peculiar sense the mediatorial kingdom has been placed in a position of abeyance or suspension during the period extending from Pentecost to the return of Christ. This means that it is not being experienced in the full sense as described in Old Testament prophecy. If it were in existence in this sense, then members of the church would be ruling on the earth (1 Cor. 4:8). In fact it would not be necessary for them to pray the prayer the Lord Jesus urged them to pray, "Thy kingdom come" (Mt. 6:10).

The proclamation of this kingdom should still be preached as Paul did (Acts 20:24-27, ASV). It is a part of the whole counsel of God. In a limited sense participation in this kingdom is being experienced by members of the church today. Upon conversion and regeneration, people are being translated into that kingdom (Col. 1:13), that is, they are becoming a part of that phase of the kingdom which will serve as the aristocracy and ruling nobility when it is fully established on the earth at the Second Coming of Christ. Thus believers actually enter the kingdom before its visible and material establishment on the earth (Jn. 3:3, 5).

The present form of the kingdom is thus described by Christ as a mystery or secret (Mt. 13:11). (I have already elaborated on this above in my discussion of the kingdom in the Gospels [p. 86].) Parallel developments to that described by Matthew 13 are taking place during this age in preparation for the kingdom. There is the preparation of a spiritual nucleus consisting of several companies of saints. These are known as the "sons of the kingdom" (Mt. 13:38). There is the church being prepared during the period from Pentecost to the rapture, and the martyrs saved during the period of tribulation (Rev. 3:21; 20:4). But in addition, during the period of the tribulation there is a great company of the saved in the natural state among whom are Jews (Rev. 7:1-8) and Gentiles (Mt. 25:34) who will go into the kingdom as the original population. Evil also develops along its own lines during the present age. "The sons of the evil one" (Mt. 13:38-39, ASV) will increase into a vast concourse of humanity that will organize into a false kingdom under the direction of Antichrist (Rev. 13:5, 7). Upon this final world empire the stone cut out of the mountain without hands will fall with crushing force and pulverize it to dust (Dan. 2:34-35, 44-45). This is the harvest at the end of the age (Rev. 14:14-20), a harvest performed by the Lord Jesus Christ, the Stone, and angelic servants (Mt. 13:36-43, 47-50). It is this concourse of events that will usher in the mediatorial kingdom of our Lord and Savior, Jesus Christ (Dan. 2:34-35, 44-45).

Realization of the Kingdom
The mediatorial kingdom will be ushered in by Christ at that point in time when he returns to the earth. The period of seven years, or slightly more, that immediately antedates this will be marked by providential and immediate judgments which will expel the usurpers from the earth. These judgments are unloosed by Christ who is in heaven holding the seven-sealed title deed to the earth in his hands. One by one he removes the seals until the judgments under the seals, the trumpets and the vials have run their course (Rev. 6—19). Then Christ returns to the earth with the church (Rev. 19: 7-8, 14) which he caught away into heaven before this awful period began (1 Thess. 4:13-17).

At this point Christ will begin to exercise the authority delegated to him (Mt. 28:18) in establishing his kingdom (Rev. 11: 15-17). The personal presence of Christ is the chief distinguishing quality of this kingdom. It is the Stone, Christ, that increases and fills the whole earth (Dan. 2:34-35, 44-45). Christ will come in glory (Mt. 24:30; 25:31) with supernatural power. He will be accompanied by the angels, and shall establish and sit upon his throne (Rev. 19:11-21). The final company of dead saints will have been raised from the dead (1 Cor. 15:23-24). The church saints will have been raised at the time of the rapture, preceding the tribulation. At the middle of the tribulation two martyred witnesses will be raised (Rev. 11:11). At the end of the tribulation the great company of tribulation martyrs will be raised (Rev. 20:4) in close proximity with the Old Testament saints (Is. 26:19-21; Dan. 12:1-2).

The mediatorial kingdom will then be realized in all of its aspects. Little is said in the New Testament about the vast changes that will occur in this realm. These must be found in Old Testament prophecy. But Christ assured believers that these changes would take place just as set forth in Old Testament prophecy (Mt. 5:17-18; Acts 3:19-26). The curse will be partially lifted, so much so that Isaiah describes the change as a new heaven and a new earth (Is. 65:17). It will be necessary to exercise a stern and inflexible rule of righteousness to control sin and perpetuate the virtues of this kingdom (Rev. 12:5; 19:15). Throughout the entire period of the mediatorial kingdom the ministry of Christ will be directed toward a progressive subjugation of all enemies to his official and personal rule (1 Cor. 15:25-26; Rev. 20:7-10; 22:2-3). When this mission is accomplished, he will then voluntarily deliver the kingdom into the hands of the Father, and the mediatorial kingdom will be merged with the universal kingdom (1 Cor. 15:24, 28) which will usher in the eternal state (Rev. 21:1-2). Then there will be but one throne through the ages of the ages (Rev. 22:1, 3).

AN HISTORIC PREMILLENNIAL RESPONSE
GEORGE ELDON LADD

Hoyt's essay reflects the major problem in the discussion of the millennium. Several times he contrasts nondispensational views with his own, which he labels "the biblical view" (pp. 69-70, 84). If he is correct, then the other views, including my own, are "unbiblical" or even heretical. This is the reason that over the years there has been little creative dialogue between dispensationalists and other schools of prophetic interpretation.

There is nothing distinctively dispensational about Hoyt's definition of the kingdom, even though it is quoted from McClain. Furthermore, his distinction between God's kingdom and his mediatorial kingdom is not the usual dispensational distinctive. In my view, God is universal King of the universe, but as his kingdom comes to men it is always *mediated* through Christ both in the present and in the future. It is also interesting to find Hoyt making no distinction between the kingdom of God and the kingdom of heaven. Walvoord, the foremost American dispensational theologian, distinguishes between the two: the kingdom of heaven is the realm of *profession*, the kingdom of God the realm of true believers.[1]

It is difficult to see how Hoyt can successfully argue that the mediatorial kingdom was "suspended" (the usual dispensational word is "postponed") when it was rejected by Israel. The fact is, Jesus' offer of the kingdom was not *universally* rejected. A good number of people received it and became Jesus' disciples. Paul speaks of an appearance of the resurrected Jesus to over five hundred brethren (1 Cor. 15:6). These constituted a "little flock" (Lk. 12:32)—an idea which often appears in the Old Testament (Israel as the flock of God's pasture). The little flock received the kingdom Jesus offered and thus became the people of the kingdom—the true spiritual Israel.

One important point prominent in dispensationalism which Hoyt downplays is the Jewishness of the millennial kingdom. True, he does say that "this kingdom will be a revival and continuation of the historical Davidic kingdom" (pp. 78-79), but he fails to emphasize that this means the rebuilding of the temple and the restoration of the entire Old Testament cult with its endless cycle of bloody sacrifices. This is made impossible by Hebrews 8:13.

One last word: Hoyt writes, "At no point does Christ ever intimate that his conception of the kingdom is any different from that in Old Testament prophecy" (p. 85). This in my view misses the central message of the Gospels. Jesus said, "But if it is by the Spirit of God that I cast out demons, then the kingdom of God has come upon you" (Mt. 12:28). Jesus claimed that in his person—a man among men—resided the power of the Holy Spirit, and its activity was nothing less than the power of the reign of God. Here is something utterly different from the prevailing Old Testament hope. Before the kingdom comes in eschatological power and glory, it has come to men in an unexpected form—in the person and message of a Nazarene teacher. This, to me, is the "mystery"—the revealed secret—of the kingdom of God.

A POSTMILLENNIAL RESPONSE
LORAINE BOETTNER

In attempting to reply to Hoyt's interpretation of the millennial kingdom I shall not deal with the individual prophecies but shall set forth some basic principles which in my opinion refute the dispensational system and show what the Bible really does teach. This disagreement arises primarily because of the different methods of interpretation. It is generally agreed that if the prophecies are taken literally, they do foretell a restoration of the nation of Israel in the land of Palestine with the Jews having a prominent place in that kingdom and ruling over the other nations.

In many of our Bibles, such as the American Standard Version of 1901, on the flyleaf between the Old and the New Testament are the words:

The New Covenant

commonly called

The New Testament

The Old Covenant was established with the nation of Israel at Mount Sinai shortly after the Israelites were delivered from Egypt. Before the Covenant was given, God, speaking through Moses, said to the people, "Now therefore, if you will obey my voice and keep my covenant, you shall be my own possession among all peoples; for all the earth is mine; and you shall be to me a kingdom of priests and a holy nation" (Ex. 19:5-6). After two days' preparation in which the people were to sanctify themselves and wash their clothes, God came down on Mount Sinai and gave the Covenant in a most impressive manner. We are told that there were thunders and lightnings, a thick cloud, a loud voice of a trumpet; the mountain smoked and quaked; the people seeing and hearing that trembled; and God spoke in an audible voice.

What we term the Old Covenant was then given, consisting primarily of the Ten Commandments, recorded in Exodus 20:1-17, together with various accompanying laws as recorded on through chapter 24—what we might term the "constitution and bylaws" by which the Israelites were to be governed the remainder of their existence as a nation.

In time that Covenant would be replaced by what would be called the New Covenant, which God would make with the church. That was predicted most fully and clearly by the prophet Jeremiah who wrote,

"Behold, the days are coming, says the LORD, when I will make a new covenant with the house of Israel and the house of Judah; not like the covenant which I made with their fathers when I took them by the hand to bring them out of the land of Egypt, my covenant which they broke, though I was their husband says the LORD. But this is the covenant which I will make with the house of Israel after those days, says the LORD: I will put my law within them, and I will write it upon their hearts; and I will be their God, and they shall be my people. And no longer shall each man teach his neighbor and each his brother, saying, 'Know the LORD,' for they shall all know me, from the least of them to the greatest, says the LORD; for I will forgive their iniquity, and I will remember their sin no more." (Jer. 31:31-34)

A most remarkable phenomenon in the science of Bible study is that only a very few of those who call themselves evangelical Christians take any notice of the fact that the Old Covenant, which we have in the first part of our Bibles in the Old Testament, was made *exclusively* with the nation of Israel and that it now has been replaced by the New Covenant, which we call the New Testament, which was made *exclusively* with the church. "I am the LORD your God, who brought you out of the land of Egypt, out of the house of bondage," said the Lord God as the Old Covenant was established with the nation of Israel (Ex. 20:2). That means Israel. Only they came out of Egypt. Hence that Covenant pointedly was *not* made with the Egyptians or the Philistines or the Persians or the Greeks. It was specifically made with one group and with them alone. However, as we find later, Gentile proselytes could come into the nation of Israel and into the covenant relationship with God, but only through certain prescribed rituals.

The New Testament, which alone is the authoritative document for the Christian church, should be called the New Covenant. *Testament,* as in "last will and testament," means dying counsel or final disposition of property. But the New Testament is not the dying counsel of Jesus. Rather it is the New Covenant which was given in fulfillment of the promise that came through Jeremiah. That was what Christ announced when he instituted the Lord's Supper. "This cup which is poured out for you is the new covenant in my blood" (Lk. 22:20).

The writer of the epistle to the Hebrews cited the promise made through Jeremiah and declared that the New Covenant had made the first Covenant old. It was even then vanishing away (Heb. 8:7-13). It would soon vanish completely with the destruction of the temple and its ritual worship, the priesthood, the genealogies, the city of Jerusalem, the devastation of the land and the dispersion of the Jews through the nations in the year A.D. 70. Thus he showed that the Old Covenant had served its purpose and that it had been replaced by the New Covenant.

In strong language Paul says that when we were dead in trespasses and sins, Christ made us "alive together with him, having forgiven us all our trespasses, having canceled the bond which stood against us with its legal demands; this he set aside, nailing it to the cross" (Col. 2:13-14). Notice those last words: "nailing it to the cross." The old order died when Christ died. No requirements from the Old Covenant are binding on the Christian except the moral principles that are repeated in the New Covenant. The Old Testament is our *history* book. It is *not* our *law book.*

It is true of course that in the Old Testament certain promises were made to Israel concerning a future regathering of the people and restoration of the land. But those promises were *always* conditioned on obedience, either expressly stated or clearly implied. Time and again the people *were warned that apostasy would cancel the promise of future blessing, that promised blessing could be forfeited.*

The land of Palestine, for instance, was given to Abraham and to his seed "for an everlasting possession" (Gen. 17:8). But the same thing is said of the perpetual duration of the priesthood of Aaron (Ex. 40:15), the Passover (Ex. 12:14), the Sabbath (Ex. 31:17) and David's throne (2 Sam. 7:13, 16, 24). But in the light of the New Testament all of those things have passed away. We use the same terminology when a title deed grants to the buyer the use of a piece of land or property "forever" or "in perpetuity." We do not mean that the buyer will actually hold it forever but that it becomes his for as long as he chooses to hold it or until conditions change. Moreover, the people were exiled from the land for seventy years during the Babylonian captivity and for nearly two thousand years between the time that Jerusalem was destroyed by the Romans until the present day state of Israel was formed. This is actually nearly twice as long as they had possessed it. How could it now be regarded as a fulfillment of the promise to Abraham if they were given possession of it only in a one thousand year millennial kingdom? Surely that promise has long since been voided so far as fleshly Israel is concerned.

When God delivered the children of Israel out of Egypt, he promised that he would bring them into "a good land and broad land, a land flowing with milk and honey" (Ex. 3:8). But when they rebelled after hearing the reports of the twelve spies, he said:

> Doubtless ye shall not come into the land, concerning which I sware to make you dwell therein, save Caleb the son of Jephunneh, and Joshua the son of Nun. But your little ones, which ye said should be a prey, them will I bring in, and they shall know the land which ye have despised. But as for you, your carcasses, they shall fall in this wilderness. . . . And ye shall know my breach of promise. (Num. 14:30-34, AV)

Immediately after the children of Israel came out of Egypt, Moses, speaking as God's prophet, gave them this apparently unconditional promise: "The Egyptians whom you see today, you shall never see again" (Ex. 14:13). But in his farewell address some forty years later, he specifically warned them of the consequences of disobedience: "And the LORD will bring you back in ships to Egypt, a journey which I promised that you should never make again; and there you shall offer yourselves for sale to your enemies as male and female slaves, but no man will buy you" (Deut. 28:68). Blessing was promised to the nation if they were obedient; but punishment was threatened, even to the destruction of the nation if they were disobedient (Deut. 28:13-25, 45-46).

Jeremiah declared clearly the conditional nature of God's promise to Israel: "And if at any time I declare concerning a nation or a kingdom that I will build and plant it, and if it does evil in my sight, not listening to my voice, then I will repent of the good which I had intended to do to it" (Jer. 18:9-10). Samuel warned the disobedient Eli: "Therefore the LORD the God of Israel declares: 'I promised that your house and the house of your father, should go in and out before me for ever'; but now the LORD declares: 'Far be it from me; for those who honor me I will honor, and those who despise me shall be lightly esteemed' " (1 Sam. 2:30). Thus the promise of blessing was forfeited, and the house of Eli was cut off, never to be restored.

Another classic example of an apparently unconditional promise was that given through the prophet Jonah: "Yet forty days, and Nineveh shall be overthrown" (Jon. 3:4). But when the people of Nineveh repented, the city was spared. Although Jonah wanted to see the city destroyed and was greatly disappointed when it was not, he did not feel that God had violated his promise, for we read:

But it displeased Jonah exceedingly, and he was angry. And he prayed to the LORD and said, "I pray thee, O LORD, is not this what I said when I was yet in my country? That is why I made haste to flee to Tarshish; for I knew that thou art a gracious God and merciful, slow to anger, and abounding in steadfast love, and repentest of evil." (4:1-2)

Numerous other such warnings might be cited. But these are sufficient to show that *no promise will be fulfilled to a disobedient and rebellious people.* It was not necessary, and it would not have been good literary form, for the sacred writer to have repeated the threat of punishment or disinheritance every time a promise was given. But it was repeated often enough that the observant reader would know that God would be under no obligation to fulfill any promise to a disobedient Israel. On this basis we have no hesitation in saying that *all of the promises made to Israel in the Old Testament either were fulfilled, or they have been forfeited through disobedience.*

Incidentally, regarding what is generally considered the most important promise that God made to Israel, namely, that they should possess all the land of Palestine, that promise was fulfilled once. It was given to Israel through Joshua's conquests. They lost it only because of their disobedience. Hence there is no reason why it should be given to them a second time. In Joshua 21:43, 45 we read: "Thus the LORD gave to Israel all the land which he swore to give to their fathers; and having taken possession of it, they settled . . . there. Not one of all the good promises which the LORD had made to the house of Israel had failed; all came to pass." And again we are told, "Solomon ruled over all the kingdoms from the Euphrates to the land of the Philistines and to the border of Egypt; they brought tribute and served Solomon all the days of his life" (1 Kings 4:21). Actually God did mercifully give them a second chance, when the captives came back from Babylon. But again they lost it through disobedience.

The fact is that when Christ came and was rejected, he deposed the leaders of apostate Judaism, the Pharisees and elders, and appointed a new set of officials, the apostles, through whom he established his church. Once he told the Jewish rulers, "The kingdom of God will be taken away from you and given to a nation producing the fruits of it" (Mt. 21:43). And because they rejected and crucified the Messiah, and persisted in opposing the church even after it was founded, they were brought into a condition in which, as Paul solemnly says, "wrath is come upon them to the uttermost" (1 Thess. 2:16, AV). That leaves no space for a future nationalistic conversion. In accordance with this the entire system of Judaism has been abrogated, finished, brought to an end; and the church has taken its place. The New Covenant is now the authoritative instrument for God's dealings with his people. This biblical doctrine of the covenants, in my opinion, renders impossible both the historic premillennial and the dispensational premillennial position. It is compatible with either the amillennial or the postmillennial position.

For information concerning the first coming of Christ, we go to the Old Testament. He came exactly as predicted, and all of those prophecies were fulfilled or were forfeited through disobedience. But for information concerning his Second Coming and what future developments will be, we go only to the New Testament.

There we learn that when he comes again he will not come to establish a kingdom. He did that at his first coming, and he is now reigning. In Mark 9:1 Jesus says, "Truly I say to you, there are some standing here who will not taste of death before they see that the kingdom of God has come with power." Hence we know that the kingdom has come—or some of those who stood there that day are still living, which certainly is not the case.

In Acts 2 we find that the kingdom did come with power at Pentecost and that the apostles were given power—power which transformed weak, frightened disciples into strong, fearless apostles who on that day and later preached the message of salvation to the nations with marvelous results. The external manifestation of that kingdom is the church. And when Christ comes again, he will not come to sit on David's throne for he is now sitting on that throne. In his sermon at Pentecost Peter declared that "the patriarch David . . . both died and was buried"; and then he adds: "Being therefore a prophet, and knowing that God had sworn with an oath to him that he would set one of his descendents upon his throne, he foresaw and spoke of the resurrection of Christ, that he was not abandoned to Hades, nor did his flesh see corruption" (Acts 2:29-32). There we are told that the purpose of Christ's resurrection was that he might sit on David's throne. And in verses 34 and 35 of that same chapter Peter, quoting Psalm

110:1, says that he is to sit on that throne and reign until all his enemies have been made the footstool of his feet.

Paul says that God the Father has "delivered us from the dominion of darkness and transferred us to the kingdom of his beloved Son" (Col. 1:13). (Note the past tense in both instances.) And John also tells us that we are now in the kingdom: "To him who loves us and has freed us from our sins by his blood and made us a kingdom...." (Rev. 1:5-6).

Hence when Christ comes again, it will not be to reign in a millennial kingdom. He is now reigning in his mediatorial kingdom. And he will not come to fight his enemies, for they shall have been defeated and vanquished before that time.

Instead we read:

Then comes the end, when he delivers the kingdom to God the Father after destroying every rule and every authority and power. For he must reign until he has put all his enemies under his feet. The last enemy to be destroyed is death. "For God has put all things in subjection under his feet." But when it says, "All things are put in subjection under him," it is plain that he is excepted who put all things under him. When all things are subjected to him, then the Son himself will also be subjected to him who put all things under him, that God may be everything to every one." (1 Cor. 15:24-28, my emphasis)

Hence when Christ comes again, it will be to merge his present mediatorial kingdom with the eternal kingdom that God the Father, God the Son and God the Holy Spirit may reign as one God throughout all eternity.

AN AMILLENNIAL RESPONSE
ANTHONY A. HOEKEMA

Though there may be many statements in Hoyt's essay with which I agree, I disagree basically with the position he has set forth. My disagreement concerns primarily his method of interpreting Scripture.

On pages 66-67 Hoyt indicates his main principle of scriptural interpretation:

This principle clearly stated is that of taking the Scriptures in their literal and normal sense, understanding that this applies to the entire Bible. This means that the historical content of the Bible is to be taken literally; the doctrinal material is also to be interpreted in this way; the moral and spiritual information likewise follows this pattern; and the prophetic material is also to be understood in this way. . . . Any other method of interpretation partially, if not completely, robs God's people of the message which was intended for them.

What makes Hoyt's essay difficult to evaluate is that he nowhere gives us a specific exegesis of any Scripture passage. Most of the time he simply gives scriptural references in parentheses; occasionally he quotes a Bible passage; but never does he give a detailed and argued interpretation of a passage. To be sure, we all do a certain amount of this kind of thing. But certainly in an essay on "Dispensational Premillennialism" one would expect at the very least a careful exegesis of Revelation 20:1-6. Hoyt simply assumes that Revelation 20 teaches an earthly millennial reign of Christ and then finds this earthly reign predicted in Old Testament prophecy. But the crucial question is, How can we be sure that Revelation 20 teaches such an earthly reign? This question he does not answer.

The only way we can surmise how Hoyt interprets the various Scripture passages he mentions is to note what he says in connection with these references. Let us now look at some of these statements to see whether he is true to his announced principle of interpretation. I found the following six instances where Hoyt failed to follow the literal method of interpretation:

1. On page 79 the author finds proof for the supernatural establishment of the mediatorial kingdom (which for him means the millennial kingdom) in Matthew 25:31-46. This interpretation, however, is not based on the literal method. For the sheep in the judgment scene are said to go away "into life eternal" (v. 46); but to enter the millennial kingdom is by no means to be equated with receiving eternal life. Are there not, according to premillennial teaching, still unregenerate people in the millennium, some of whom will rebel against Christ at the end of the millennial period and be sent to perdition?

2. On page 84 Hoyt says, "Certain expressions mark the nearness of this kingdom. Christ is set forth as its source of power (Lk. 11:20). This is explained by the fact that the King was standing in their midst (Lk. 17:21, ASV marg.)." But these passages say that the *kingdom* has come upon them (Lk. 11:20) and that the *kingdom of God* is within them or in the midst of them (Lk. 17:21); not just that the *king* is standing in their midst.

3. On page 86 the author affirms that the treasure hid in a field mentioned by Jesus in Matthew 13:44 is Israel, and that the pearl of great price of Matthew 13:45-46 is the church. But where is this identification mentioned in Scripture? Is this "literal interpretation"?

4. On page 87 Hoyt says that during his trial Jesus continued to urge his claims as the mediatorial King of Old Testament prophecy—meaning (I infer from the earlier part of the essay) the King of an earthly kingdom which would involve sitting on an earthly throne and ruling over Israel. One of the passages quoted in support of this statement is John 18:33-39. But in the course of this dialogue with Pilate Jesus says, "My kingdom is not of this world: if my kingdom were of this world, then would my servants fight . . . but now is my kingdom not from hence" (Jn. 18:36, AV). When Pilate then asks Jesus, "Art thou a king then?" Jesus answers, "Thou sayest that I am a king. To this end was I born, and for this cause came I into the world, that I should bear witness unto the truth" (Jn. 18:37, AV).

Surely Jesus' replies to Pilate indicate that he is not the King of an earthly kingdom but that he is King in the realm of truth —in other words, the King of a kingdom which is primarily spiritual, not earthly.

5. On page 89 the author says, "At last the apostles were forced to turn from the Jews to the Gentiles with their message of Christ and his kingdom." For proof he adduces, among other passages, Acts 19:8-9 and 28:17-31. Both of these passages, however, show Paul bringing the "message of Christ and his kingdom" to Jews.

6. On page 92 Hoyt says that Christ "shall establish and sit upon his throne (Rev. 19:11-21)." But the passage does not mention a throne; it describes Christ as sitting on a horse.

In all six of these instances the author has not followed his own principle of interpretation, that of "taking the Scriptures in their literal and normal sense." Other instances could be noted, but these are enough to show that it is a gross oversimplification to suggest that the main issue between dispensationalists and nondispensationalists is that of a literal versus a nonliteral interpretation of Scripture. Dispensationalists sometimes interpret nonliterally, and nondispensationalists sometimes interpret literally.

The crucial question is, Is dispensational premillennialism based on a sound method of interpreting Scripture? To that question my answer is, No.

The really basic interpretative principle underlying Hoyt's essay seems to be this: The Old Testament provides the key for the interpretation of the New Testament. Hoyt builds his case for the future restoration of Israel as a nation primarily on Old Testament prophecies and then proceeds to interpret the New Testament in the light of his literal interpretation of these Old Testament prophecies. But he ignores New Testament teachings which show that the future of believing Israel is not to be separated from the future of believing non-Israelites.

The New Testament itself, however, indicates that Christ and the apostles are the authoritative interpreters of the Old Testament. The book of Hebrews gives us the key to this revelatory principle: "God, who at sundry times and in divers manners spake in time past unto the fathers by the prophets, hath in these last days spoken unto us by his Son" (Heb. 1:1-2, AV). Christ told his disciples before he left them: "I will not leave you comfortless: I will come to you" (Jn. 14:18, AV). From the previous two verses we learn that he will come to them and remain with them through the Holy Spirit whom the Father will give them. Later in the same discourse Jesus tells his disciples, "All things that the Father hath are mine: therefore said I, that he shall take of mine, and shall shew it unto you" (Jn. 16:15, AV). What can this mean but that the

Holy Spirit shall now lead the disciples, who along with Paul are to be the main authors of the New Testament Scriptures, into a deeper and more accurate understanding of the truth about Christ's mission and work? In agreement with this, Luke tells us in Acts 1:1, "The former treatise have I made, O Theophilus, of all that Jesus began both to do and teach," clearly implying that the book which he is now writing will tell about what Jesus continued to do and teach. Paul corroborates this point when he tells the Galatians that the gospel which he preached to them was not after man, since he received it "by the revelation of Jesus Christ" (Gal. 1:11-12, AV). From all these passages it is clear that what the apostles teach us about how the Old Testament prophecies are to be understood is authoritative for us since they were taught by Christ through the Spirit sent by him.

The following five major teachings of dispensational premillennialism, as found in Hoyt's essay, should be rejected as not in harmony with Scripture:

1. *The Old Testament predicts Christ's millennial reign.* This is obviously Hoyt's position since many, if not most, of the passages he adduces to describe this millennial reign are taken from the Old Testament. As a matter of fact, however, the Old Testament says nothing about such a millennial reign. Passages quoted or referred to by Hoyt as describing this millennial reign actually describe the new earth or the final state of blessedness.

So, for example, on page 92 the author quotes what Isaiah 65:17 says about the new heaven and the new earth as referring to the millennial kingdom. But obviously this expression refers to the final state, not the millennium, as is evident from the use of these words in Revelation 21:1. How, in fact, can it be a *new* earth when the curse will be only *partially* lifted (p. 92)? On page 82 it is said that in the millennial kingdom war will be completely eliminated, with a reference to Isaiah 2:4.

But according to dispensational teaching war will not be completely eliminated from the millennium since the great battle of Gog and Magog described in Revelation 20 must still take place! Only on the new earth will Isaiah's prophecy about the end of war be fulfilled. Another feature of the millennial kingdom is that "Israel will be restored permanently to her land" (p. 83); the passage quoted in support of this is Amos 9:14-15. But that passage says that Israel "shall no more be pulled up out of their land" (AV). What is pictured here is not just a dwelling in the land for a thousand-year period, but for all time. These words are a description of the new earth, not just of the millennial kingdom.

2. *There is a sharp separation between Israel and the church in God's redemptive program, so that Israel is said to have a future quite distinct from the future of the church.* But the New Testament clearly shows that the middle wall of partition between believing Gentiles and believing Jews has been broken down (Eph. 2:14), that God has reconciled both Jews and Gentiles unto himself "in one body" (Eph. 2:16), and that therefore believing Gentiles now belong to the same household of God to which believing Jews belong (Eph. 2:19). Similarly in Romans 11, where Paul describes incorporation into the fellowship of God's people in terms of being grafted into a tree, that fellowship is pictured not in terms of two trees (one Jewish and one Gentile) but of *one olive tree* (Rom. 11:17-24). And Peter, in words which are an obvious echo of Exodus 19: 5-6, applies words to the New Testament church (consisting of both Jews and Gentiles) which were originally spoken to Israel: "Ye are a chosen generation, a royal priesthood, an holy nation, a peculiar people" (1 Pet. 2:9). This indicates that the New Testament church is now indeed the spiritual Israel, the people of God's possession. If the church is now indeed *God's holy nation*, what room is left for the emergence of another holy nation, distinct from the church?

3. *Old Testament prophecies about Israel are always interpreted literally.* The New Testament itself rejects this principle. For an example let us see how Amos 9:11 is interpreted in Acts 15. Amos 9:11 reads, "In that day will I raise up the tabernacle of David that is fallen" (AV). These words might be interpreted to mean that at some time in the future there will be a restoration, in terms of an earthly reign, of the kingdom of David which now lies in ruins. This is, in fact, the way Hoyt interprets the passage (pp. 78-79, with reference to Acts 15: 16-18). But let us take a closer look at the passage in Acts. The scene is the so-called "Council of Jerusalem." First Peter and then Paul and Barnabas tell how God has brought Gentiles to the faith through their ministry. Now James gets up and says,

> Simeon hath declared how God at the first did visit the Gentiles, to take out of them a people for his name. And to this agree the words of the prophets; as it is written, after this I will return, and will build again the tabernacle of David, which is fallen down; and I will build again the ruins thereof, and I will set it up: that the residue of men might seek after the Lord, and all the Gentiles, upon whom my name is called, saith the Lord, who doeth all these things. (Acts 15:14-17, AV)

James is saying that the wonderful thing which is now happening, namely, that Gentiles are now coming into the fellowship of God's people, is a fulfillment of the words of the prophet Amos about the building up again of the fallen tabernacle of David. In other words, the fallen tabernacle of David is being built up not in a material way (by means of a restored earthly kingdom) but in a spiritual way (as Gentiles are coming into the kingdom of God). The words "after this" are not a reference to an event still in the future but are simply a translation of Amos's words, "In that day." That day is now! Here is a clear instance in which the New Testament "spiritualizes" or interprets figuratively an Old Testament prophecy about the tabernacle or kingdom of David.

Other examples could be given. Martin Wyngaarden has pointed out in his book, *The Future of the Kingdom* (Baker, 1955), that the New Testament frequently gives a figurative interpretation of such concepts as the following: Zion, Jerusalem, the Holy Land, the kingdom, the seed of Abraham, Israel, the sacrifices and the temple.

4. *There is a future centrality for Israel as a nation.* On page 77 Hoyt quotes Acts 1:6 as proving that the mediatorial kingdom will be restored (meaning a restoration of national Israel). But what we have in Acts 1:6 is a question: "Lord, wilt thou at this time restore again the kingdom to Israel?" (AV). Jesus answers the disciples: "It is not for you to know the times or the seasons, which the Father hath put in his own power. But ye shall receive power, after that the Holy Ghost is come upon you: and ye shall be witnesses unto me . . ." (Acts 1:7-8, AV). One could say, I suppose, that Jesus' answer to their question leaves room for the possibility that the kingdom would indeed be restored to Israel in the sense in which the disciples expected this to happen. One could also say that Jesus' answer turns their thoughts in a different direction: witnessing to all peoples rather than waiting for a restored Israelitish kingdom. In any event, the mere fact that the disciples ask this question does not prove that what they are asking for will happen.

But why does Hoyt not quote Jesus' words as recorded in Matthew 21:43, "Therefore say I unto you, The kingdom of God shall be taken from you [the chief priests, the elders and the Pharisees to whom he is speaking, who represent the nation of Israel], and given to a nation bringing forth the fruits thereof" (AV)? Nowhere in the New Testament do we read that these words were ever revoked. Jesus' words do not mean that there is no possibility of salvation for Jews, but they do rule out a future centrality of the Jewish nation. Even if one understands Paul's words in Romans 11:26 ("and so all Israel will be saved") as teaching a future conversion of Israel (and I am not convinced that they do), they still say nothing about the nation of Israel as a political unit—or about Palestine or about Jerusalem. What Paul is saying in chapters 9 through 11 of Romans is that Israelites can be saved in the same way that non-Israelites can be saved, namely, by faith in Christ (see Rom. 11:23).

The New Testament does not predict a future restoration of Israel as a nation but finds the promises to Israel fulfilled in the resurrection of Jesus Christ and in the forgiveness of sins which one can obtain through Christ. This is shown by Paul in his sermon to the Jews gathered in the synagogue of Antioch in Pisidia:

> We declare unto you glad tidings, how that the promise which was made unto the fathers, God hath fulfilled the same unto us their children, in that he hath raised up Jesus again; as it is also written in the second psalm, Thou art my Son, this day have I begotten thee. And as concerning that he raised him up from the dead, now no more to return to corruption, he said on this wise, I will give you the sure mercies of David. . . . Be it known unto you therefore, men and brethren, that through this man is preached unto you the forgiveness of sins. (Acts 13:32-34, 38, AV)

5. *The mediatorial kingdom of God is only future.* On page 91, after summarizing a number of events which will precede Christ's Second Coming, Hoyt says, "It is this concourse of events that will usher in the mediatorial kingdom of our Lord and Savior, Jesus Christ." In other words, the mediatorial kingdom of Christ will not begin until he comes again. To be sure, I would reply, the kingdom of God as described in Scripture does have a future phase. But to say that it is *only future* and to deny that the mediatorial kingdom began at the time of

Christ's first coming is to be guilty of a serious distortion of biblical teaching.

Let us look at some of the words of Jesus on this matter. According to Matthew 12:28 Jesus said to the Pharisees, "But if I cast out devils by the Spirit of God, then the kingdom of God is come unto you" (AV). In Luke 17:20-21 Jesus is quoted as saying, again to the Pharisees, "The kingdom of God cometh not with observation: Neither shall they say, Lo here! or lo there! for, behold, the kingdom of God is within you" (AV; other versions have "among you" or "in the midst of you"). In the Sermon on the Mount, the beatitudes describe the kind of people of whom it may be said, "theirs is the kingdom of heaven" (Mt. 5:3). When the disciples ask Jesus a question about who is the greatest in the kingdom of heaven, Jesus asks a child to join the group and says, "Whosoever therefore shall humble himself as this little child, the same is greatest in the kingdom of heaven" (Mt. 18:4, AV). And when the disciples were rebuking those who were bringing children to Jesus, Jesus said, "Let the children come to me, and do not hinder them; for to such belongs the kingdom of heaven" (Mt. 19:14). All of these passages show that the kingdom of God or of heaven was present already when Jesus was on earth.

That the kingdom of God is a present as well as a future reality is also evident from the words of Paul. In 1 Corinthians 4:19-20 we hear him saying, "But I will come to you shortly, if the Lord will, and will know, not the speech of them which are puffed up, but the power. For the kingdom of God is not in word, but in power" (AV). In Romans 14:17 Paul writes, "For the kingdom of God is not meat and drink; but righteousness, and peace and joy in the Holy Ghost" (AV). And in Colossians 1:13 Paul sums up the privileged status of believers by saying that God the Father "hath delivered us from the power of darkness, and hath translated us into the kingdom of his dear Son" (AV).

Both Jesus and Paul also speak of the kingdom in its future aspect. But it is obvious from the words quoted above that they clearly taught the presence of the kingdom in their time. To hold that the mediatorial kingdom is only future, therefore, is to fail to do justice to clear New Testament teachings.

III
POSTMILLENNIALISM

POSTMILLENNIALISM
LORAINE BOETTNER

Postmillennialism is that view of the last things which holds that the kingdom of God is now being extended in the world through the preaching of the gospel and the saving work of the Holy Spirit in the hearts of individuals, that the world eventually is to be Christianized and that the return of Christ is to occur at the close of a long period of righteousness and peace commonly called the millennium.[1] It should be added that on postmillennial principles the Second Coming of Christ will be followed immediately by the general resurrection, the general judgment, and the introduction of heaven and hell in their fullness.

The millennium to which the postmillennialist looks forward is thus a golden age of spiritual prosperity during this present dispensation, that is, during the Church Age. This is to be brought about through forces now active in the world. It is to last an indefinitely long period of time, perhaps much longer than a literal one thousand years. The changed character of individuals will be reflected in an uplifted social, economic, political and cultural life of mankind. The world at large will then enjoy a state of righteousness which up until now has been seen only in relatively small and isolated groups: for example, some family circles, and some local church groups and kindred organizations.

This does not mean that there will be a time on this earth when every person will be a Christian or that all sin will be abolished. But it does mean that evil in all its many forms eventually will be reduced to negligible proportions, that Christian principles will be the rule, not the exception, and that Christ will return to a truly Christianized world.

Postmillennialism further holds that the universal proclamation of the gospel and the ultimate conversion of the large majority of men in all nations during the present dispensation was the express command, meaning and promise of the Great Commission given by Christ himself when he said,

All authority in heaven and on earth has been given to me. Go therefore and make disciples of all nations, baptizing them in the name of the Father and of the Son and of the Holy Spirit, teaching them to observe all that I have commanded you; and lo, I am with you always, to the close of the age. (Mt. 28:18-20)

We believe that the Great Commission includes not merely the formal and external announcement of the gospel preached as a "witness" to the nations, as the premillennialists and amillennialists hold, but the true and effectual evangelization of all the nations so that the hearts and lives of the people are transformed by it. That seems quite clear from the fact that all authority in heaven and on earth and an endless sweep or conquest has been given to Christ, and through him to his disciples specifically for that purpose. They were commanded not merely to preach but to make disciples of all the nations. It was no doubtful experiment to which they were called, but to a sure triumph. The preaching of the gospel under the direction of the Holy Spirit during this dispensation is, therefore, the all-sufficient means for accomplishing that purpose.

We must acknowledge that the church during the past nineteen centuries has been extremely negligent in her duty and that the crying need of our time is for her to take seriously the task assigned to her. Instead of discussions of social, economic and political problems, book reviews and entertaining platitudes from the pulpit, the need is for sermons with real gospel content, designed to change lives and to save souls. The charge of negligence applies, of course, not only to ministers but equally to the laity. Every individual Christian is called to give his witness and to show his faith by personal testimony, through the distribution of the printed word, or through the generous and effective use of his time and money for Christian purposes. Christ commanded the evangelization of the world. That is our task. Surely he will not, and in fact cannot, come back and say to his church, "Well done, good and faithful servant," until that task has been accomplished. Rev. J. Marcellus Kik has said:

That there is still a remnant of paganism and papalism in the world is chiefly the fault of the Church. The Word of God is just as powerful in our generation as it was during the early history of the Church. The power of the Gospel is just as strong in this century as in the days of the Reformation. These enemies could be completely vanquished if the Christians of this day and age were as vigorous, as bold, as earnest, as prayerful, and as faithful as Christians were in the first several centuries and in the time of the Reformation.[2]

It should be remembered, however, that while post-, a- and premillennialists differ in regard to the manner and time of Christ's return, that is, in regard to the events that are to precede or follow his return, they agree that he will return personally, visibly and in great glory. Each alike looks for the "blessed hope, the appearing of the glory of our great God and our Savior Jesus Christ" (Tit. 2:13). Each acknowledges

Paul's statement that, "the Lord himself will descend from heaven, with a cry of command, with the archangel's call, and with the sound of the trumpet of God" (1 Thess. 4:16). Christ's return is taught so clearly and so repeatedly in Scripture that there can be no question in this regard for those who accept the Bible as the Word of God. They also agree that at his coming he will raise the dead, execute judgment and eventually institute the eternal state. No one of these views has an inherent liberalizing tendency. Hence the matters on which they agree are much more important than those on which they differ. This should enable them to cooperate as evangelicals and to present a united front against modernists and liberals who more or less consistently deny the supernatural throughout the whole range of Bible truth.

Inadequate Terminology
One difficulty that we constantly face in this discussion is that of an inadequate terminology. The use of prefixes *pre-* and *post-*, as attached to the word *millennial*, is to some extent unfortunate and misleading. For the distinction involves a great deal more than merely "before" or "after." The millennium expected by the premillennialist is quite a different thing from that expected by the postmillennialist. It is different not only in regard to the time and manner in which it will be set up but primarily in regard to the nature of the kingdom and the manner in which Christ exercises his control.

The postmillennialist looks for a golden age that will not be essentially different from our own so far as the basic facts of life are concerned. This age gradually merges into the millennial age as an increasing proportion of the world's inhabitants are converted to Christianity. Marriage and the home will continue, and new members will enter the human race through the natural process of birth, as at present. Sin will not be eliminated but will be reduced to a minimum as the moral and spiritual environment of the earth becomes predominantly Christian. Social, economic and educational problems will remain but with their unpleasant features greatly eliminated and their desirable features heightened. Christian principles of belief and conduct will be the accepted standards. Life during the millennium will compare with life in the world today in much the same way that life in a Christian community compares with that in a pagan or irreligious community. The church, much more zealous in her testimony to the truth and much more influential in the lives of the people, will continue to be then, as now, the outward and visible manifestation of the kingdom of God on earth. And the millennium will close with the Second Coming of Christ, the resurrection and final judgment. In short, postmillennialists set forth a spiritual kingdom in the hearts of men.

On the other hand the millennium expected by the premillennialist involves the personal, visible reign of Christ the King in Jerusalem. The kingdom is to be established not by the conversion of individual souls over a long period of time but suddenly and by overwhelming power. The Jews are to be converted not as individuals, as will those in other groups of the population, but en masse at the mere sight of Christ. They are to become the chief rulers in the new kingdom. Nature is to share in the millennial blessings and is to become abundantly productive. Even the ferocious nature of the wild beasts is to be tamed. Evil, however, does not cease to exist, nor is it necessarily decreased in amount. But it is held in check by the rod-of-iron rule of Christ. At the end of the millennium it breaks out in a terrible rebellion that all but overwhelms the saints and the holy city. During the millennium the saints in glorified bodies mingle freely with men who are still in the flesh.

This element in particular seems to present an inconsistency—a mongrel kingdom, the new earth and glorified sin-

less humanity mingling with the old earth and sinful humanity; Christ and the saints in immortal resurrection bodies
living in a world that still contains much sin and scenes of
death and decay. To bring Christ and the saints to live again in
the sinful environment of this world would seem to be the
equivalent of introducing sin into heaven. As the amillennialist William J. Grier has observed, such a company would
indeed be a "mixtum gatherum."

Amillennialists, of course, reject both the post- and the
premillennial conception. They are usually content to say that
there will be no millennium at all in either sense of the word.

The terms are, therefore, somewhat inaccurate and misleading. For that reason some theologians hesitate to label
themselves either post-, a- or premillennial. But no more
appropriate terms are available. They serve at least to distinguish the different schools of thought, and the meaning is
generally understood.

But while the three schools differ in regard to the meaning
of the word *millennium*, that does not mean that the word itself
is meaningless nor that the distinctions between the systems
are imaginary or unimportant. Quite the contrary. Actually
these systems represent widely divergent views concerning
this very important subject which, as we shall see, have far-
reaching consequences.

A broader and perhaps more accurate terminology has
been suggested by some—that of Chiliasts and Anti-Chiliasts.
Chiliasts would then include both historic premillennialists
and dispensationalists, while Anti-Chiliasts would include
both post- and amillennialists without making it necessary to
choose between these.

Furthermore, the fact that some who designate themselves
amillennialists hold that the present Church Age constitutes
the millennium and that Christ will come at the close of the
Church Age might seem to make them postmillennialists. But

since the primary tenet of postmillennialism, as generally understood, is that the coming of Christ is to follow a golden age of righteousness and peace, those who look upon the entire Church Age as the millennium are not commonly referred to as postmillennialists.

A Redeemed World

Postmillennialism places a strong emphasis on the universality of Christ's work of redemption. Hope is held out for the salvation of an incredibly large number of the race of mankind. Since it was the world, or the race, which fell in Adam, it was the world, or the race, which was the object of Christ's redemption. This does not mean that every individual will be saved but that the race, as a race, will be saved. Jehovah is no mere tribal deity, but is described as "a great king over all the earth" and "the Lord of all the earth" (Ps. 47:2; 97:5). The salvation that he had in view cannot be limited to a small, select group or favored few. The good news of redemption was not merely local news for a few villages in Palestine but was a world message; and the abundant and continuous testimony of Scripture is that the kingdom of God is to *fill* the earth, "from sea to sea, and from the River to the ends of the earth" (Zech. 9:10).

The writer of the Apocalypse says,

I looked, and behold, a great multitude which no man could number, from every nation, from all tribes and peoples and tongues, standing before the throne and before the Lamb, clothed in white robes, with palm branches in their hands, and crying out with a loud voice, saying, "Salvation belongs to our God who sits upon the throne, and to the Lamb." (Rev. 7:9-10)

God has chosen to redeem untold millions of the human race. Just what proportion has been included in his purposes of mercy, we have not been informed; but in view of the future days of prosperity which are promised to the church, it may be inferred that the great majority will eventually be found among that number. Assuming that those who die in infancy are saved, as most churches have taught and as most theologians have believed, already the larger proportion of the human race has been saved.

The idea that the saved shall far outnumber the lost is also carried out in the contrasts drawn in Scripture. Heaven is uniformly pictured as the next world, as a great kingdom, a country, a city; while on the other hand hell is uniformly represented as a comparatively small place: a prison, a lake (of fire and brimstone), a pit (perhaps deep, but narrow—see Lk. 20:35; Rev. 21:1; Mt. 5:3; Heb. 11:16; 1 Pet. 3:19; Rev. 19:20; 21:8-16). When the angels and saints are mentioned in Scripture they are said to be hosts, myriads, an innumerable multitude, ten thousand times ten thousand and many more thousands of thousands (Lk. 2:13; Is. 6:3; Rev. 5:11). But no such language is ever used in regard to the lost. By contrast their number appears to be relatively insignificant. The description of the great white throne judgment as found in Revelation 20:11-15 closes with the statement, "And if any one's name was not found written in the book of life, he was thrown into the lake of fire." This language indicates that in the judgment the norm will be to have one's name written in the book of life. Such language implies that those whose names are not written there are the exceptional—we may even say, rare—cases.

"The circle of God's election," says Dr. W. G. T. Shedd in volume 2 of his *Dogmatic Theology*, "is a great circle of the heavens and not that of a treadmill. The kingdom of Satan is insignificant in contrast with the kingdom of Christ. In the immense range of God's dominion, good is the rule, and evil is the exception. Sin is a speck upon the azure of eternity; a spot upon the sun. Hell is only a corner of the universe."

Judging from these considerations it appears, if we may hazard a guess, that the number of those who are saved may eventually bear a similar proportion to those who are lost as the number of free citizens in our commonwealth today bears to those who are in prisons and penitentiaries. Or the company of the saved may be likened to the main stalk of the tree which grows and flourishes while the lost are but as the small limbs and prunings which are cut off and destroyed in the fires. This is the prospect that postmillennialism is able to offer. Who even among those holding other systems would not wish that it were true?

Spiritual Advancement in the World

The redemption of the world is a long, slow process, extending through the centuries, yet surely approaching an appointed goal. We live in the day of advancing victory although there are many apparent setbacks. From the human point of view it often looks as though the forces of evil are about to gain the upper hand. Periods of spiritual advance and prosperity alternate with periods of spiritual decline and depression. But as one age succeeds another there is progress.

Looking back across the nearly two thousand years that have passed since the coming of Christ we can see that there has indeed been marvelous progress. This process will ultimately be completed, and before Christ comes again we shall see a Christianized world. This does not mean that all sin will ever be eradicated. There always will be some tares among the wheat until the time of harvest—and the harvest, the Lord tells us, is the end of the world. Even the righteous fall, sometimes grievously, into temptation and sin. But it does mean that Christian principles of life and conduct are to become the accepted standards in public and private life.

That a great spiritual advance has been made should be clear to all. Consider, for instance, the awful moral and spiritual conditions that existed on earth before the coming of Christ—the world at large groping helplessly in pagan darkness with slavery, polygamy, oppressed conditions of women and children, the almost complete lack of political freedom, the ignorance, poverty, and primitive medical care that was the lot of nearly all except those who belonged to the ruling classes.

Today the world at large is on a far higher plane. Christian principles are the accepted standards in many nations even though they are not consistently practiced. Slavery and polygamy have practically disappeared. The status of women and children has been improved immeasurably. Social and economic conditions in almost all nations have reached a new level. A spirit of cooperation is much more manifest among the nations than it has ever been before. International incidents which only a few years ago would have resulted in wars are now usually settled by arbitration.

As an evidence of international good will, witness the fact that the United States in a recent fiscal year appropriated more than $3 billion for the foreign aid and mutual security program. Since the end of World War 2 it has given to other nations more than $160 billion for these purposes. Since our population is approximately 210,000,000, this means an average contribution of $800.00 for every man, woman and child in the United States. And this does not include the other very considerable sums that have been given by individuals, churches and other organizations. This huge amount of goods and services has been given freely by this enlightened and predominantly Protestant nation to nations of other races and religions, with no expectation that it ever will be paid back —an effective expression of unselfishness and international good will. That record has never been even remotely approached before by this or any other nation in all the history of the world.

The London Times, one of the leading newspapers in England, after commending the wisdom and generosity with which the United States acted, said,

There are other things so obvious to us that we take them for granted. But because silence can be misunderstood it is worth saying once again that no nation has ever come into possession of such power for good or ill, for freedom or tyranny, for friendship or enmity among the peoples of the world, and that no nation in history has used those powers, by and large, with greater vision, restraint, responsibility and courage.

Today there is much more wealth consecrated to the service of the church than ever before; and, in spite of the defection toward modernism in some places, there seems to be far more really earnest evangelistic and missionary activity than at any time in the past. This is indicated by a number of developments. I cite particularly the following.

Up until the time of the Reformation, the Bible had been a book for priests only. It was written in Latin, and the Roman Church refused to allow it to be translated into the languages of the common people. But when the Reformers came on the scene all that was changed. The Bible was soon translated into all of the vernacular tongues of Europe, and wherever the light of the Reformation went it became the book of the common people. Decrees of popes and church councils gave way to the Word of life. Luther translated the entire Bible into German for the people of his native land, and within twenty-five years of its appearance one hundred editions of the German Bible came off the press. The same was true in France, Holland, England and Scotland. Protestant Bible societies now circulate more Bibles each year than were circulated in the fifteen centuries that preceded the Reformation.

Today the Bible is available in whole or in part in the native tongue of ninety-eight per cent of the people of the world.

Surely that must be acknowledged as great progress and as a very broad and substantial basis on which to rear the future structure of Christianity. None of the so-called "best sellers" attain more than a small fraction of the number of Bibles sold.

Furthermore, the Christian message is being broadcast by radio in all of the principal languages of the world. Several evangelical radio programs, with nationwide or worldwide coverage, have been launched within recent years—for example, the Lutheran Hour (Missouri Synod) with an estimated 22,000,000 listeners each week in the worldwide broadcast in more than fifty languages, The Back to God Hour (Christian Reformed Church), and The Hour of Decision (independent), to name only a few. There are literally hundreds of other Christian radio programs reaching more limited areas, some of which are heard daily. The gospel is thus brought into many a home, into many a sick room, to many a distant farm or lonely mining or lumber camp, to people on the highways and to ships at sea where it would not be otherwise heard. How marvelous that is compared with the very limited proclamation that prevailed for so many centuries! The overall result is that for the first time in history the people of the entire world have the evangelical Christian message made available to them.

The number of theological seminaries, Bible institutes and Christian colleges in which the Bible is studied systematically is growing faster than the population, and enrollment is increasing steadily. Numerous Christian magazines with very wide circulation have been established within recent years. A considerable proportion of the new books that come from the press either deal directly with Christianity or with some phase of religion.

Statistics indicate that the world over, Christianity has grown more in the last one hundred years than in the preceding eighteen hundred. It now has almost as many nominal adherents as the combined total of any other two world religions. These figures show that there are approximately 968,000,000 Christians, 276,000,000 Confucianists (including Taoists), 513,000,000 Moslems, 516,000,000 Hindus, 224,000,000 Buddhists, 63,000,000 Shintoists and 14,000,000 Jews. And while many of those who are counted as Christians are only "nominally" such, the proportion of true Christians probably is as great or greater than is the proportion of true adherents in any of the pagan religions. All of the other religions, with the exception of Islam, are much older than Christianity. All of the false religions are dying. Christianity alone is able to grow and flourish under modern civilization, while all of the others soon disintegrate when brought under its glaring light.

I am perfectly confident in asserting that all of the anti-Christian religions and anti-Christian philosophies of our day are demonstrably false. Their histories show what complete failures they have been in raising the moral, spiritual and intellectual standards of their adherents. They await only the coup de grace of an aroused and energetic Christianity to send them into oblivion. In this connection Dr. Albertus Pieters has well said,

> In the early church Ebionitism, Gnosticism, Montanism, Arianism and Pelagianism endangered the life of the church. They are remembered now only by church historians. Later it was Romanism and Socinianism. In modern life it is Unitarianism, Modernism, Mormonism, Russellism, Christian Science, Spiritualism, etc.,—a long list of movements of Satanic origin that comes on like a flood, and for a time makes timid believers afraid that the church will be overwhelmed and the gospel permanently lost to the world—but it never comes to pass. The present heresies will disappear as did those of the past.[3]

Only within the last one hundred years have foreign missions really come into their own. As they have recently been developed, with great church organizations behind them and with extensive facilities for translating and publishing Christian literature in many languages, they are in a position to carry on a work of evangelism in foreign lands such as the world has never seen before. It is safe to say that the present generation living in India, China, Japan, Korea, Indochina and the Near East has seen greater changes in religion, society and government than occurred in the preceding two thousand years. Not only has the foundation been laid in most of these countries for a further evangelical advance, but under the benign influence of the church, innumerable local churches, schools and hospitals have been founded, ethical culture and social services have advanced greatly, and moral standards are much higher than when the church was first established.

We should point out that some postmillennial writers, as well as others have fallen into the error of assuming too rapid progress. Dr. Snowden, for instance, after showing so clearly the error of the premillennialists in date setting and in assuming the near return of Christ, went on to make the same kind of an error in assuming that the millennium was just about to dawn. In his book *The Coming of the Lord* he assumed that the First World War, then in progress, would come to a successful conclusion in the near future, would put an end to militarism forever and would be followed by a rapid development toward the millennial era. That the lessons learned from the First World War should have had that effect we readily agree. But whether the time will be long or short we have no way of knowing. This we can say: Postmillennialism does not despair of the power of the gospel to convert the world but holds rather that it cannot be defeated, that over the centuries it will win its way and that eventually the goal will be achieved.

The great material prosperity of which the Bible speaks as accompanying the millennial era will be, to a large extent, the natural result of the high moral and spiritual life of that time. These blessings too are from God. In numerous prophecies temporal blessings are expressly represented as following in the train of the new covenant blessings. Surely it need not be doubted that when the other characteristics of the millennial era are realized, this material prosperity will also find its place. Godliness and sober living in a real sense bring their own reward. "Seek ye first the kingdom of God, and his righteousness; and all these things shall be added unto you," said Jesus (Mt. 6:33, AV). "Godliness is of value in every way, as it holds promise for the present life and also for the life to come" (1 Tim. 4:8). "The wilderness and the dry land shall be glad; the desert shall rejoice and blossom" (Is. 35:1).

Man's proper management of the earth, the task assigned to him before the Fall, will go far toward restoring a profitable plant and animal life. Remedy the sin condition in man and a marvelous transformation will take place in nature. Luther Burbank and others have done much to bring back many varieties of plants and fruits to their original condition which in their wild and neglected state had degenerated until they were practically worthless.

A revolution has occurred in transportation, communications, home furnishings and other areas within our own lifetime. Our modes of travel and transportation have changed more within the last hundred and fifty years than in the preceding two thousand. George Washington, using the horse-drawn stagecoach (the best means of transportation available in his day) traveled in much the same manner as did the ancient Persians and Egyptians. Automobiles, hard-surface highways, electrical power, air travel, radio, television and so on are all comparatively new. And now the new sciences of atomic and solar energy with the prospect for extremely cheap power, and the whole new field of electronics, in which we have as yet hardly more than scratched the surface, give great promise for the future. A leading industrialist recently said, "America is about to enter a new golden age of prosperity which will hinge upon the harnessing of the atom, and the advent of the electronic age." One new discovery follows another, and we see more and more clearly the tremendous potentials that are available for good, potentials that through all these many centuries have remained largely unused.

Knowledge has become very widespread. Schools, even for advanced study, have been made available for all classes of people. Books, magazines, newspapers, libraries, scientific laboratories and so on make available vast stores of knowledge that only two or three generations ago were confined almost exclusively to favored, limited groups.

In the administration of justice great progress has been made as Christian principles have gained wider acceptance. British and American justice today is world-renowned for its meticulous consideration for the rights of the accused and of prisoners.

But no matter how marvelous this material prosperity may become, it will ever remain but the by-product of the moral and spiritual prosperity that already to some extent characterizes the partially Christianized nations. It is abundantly clear that these blessings do not originate under pagan religions. Many nations that are the victims of those religions have lain in their poverty and ignorance and moral degradation for centuries or even for thousands of years while making practically no progress. The progress that has already occurred, originating largely in the Protestant nations of Western Europe and the United States, has been achieved in connection with only a limited amount of progress toward the millennium. What marvels must lie ahead when nations the world over are Christian—when the millennium becomes a reality!

The golden age of righteousness is, of course, not to be thought of as beginning suddenly or on any particular date. It cannot be pinpointed on the calendar for it comes as the result of a long, slow process. "The kingdom of heaven is not coming with signs to be observed" (Lk. 17:20). It is "first the blade, then the ear, then the full grain in the ear" (Mk. 4:28). Or again, it is "precept upon precept, precept upon precept, line upon line, line upon line; here a little, there a little" (Is. 28:10).

The coming of the millennium is like the coming of summer, although ever so much more slowly and on a much grander scale. In the struggle between the seasons there are many advances and many apparent setbacks. Time and again the first harbingers of spring appear only to be overcome by the winter winds. It often seems that the struggle has been lost and that the cold of winter will never be broken. But gradually the moderate spring breezes take over, and after a time we find ourselves in the glorious summer season.

Trying to pinpoint the date on which the millennium begins is like trying to distinguish the day or year when medieval history ended and modern history began. The discovery of America by Columbus usually is taken as the landmark dividing the two. At least for Americans that is where medievalism ends and where the story of America begins. But that discovery made no immediate changes in the life of the world, and in fact Columbus himself died without ever knowing that he had discovered a new world. In retrospect and for convenience we arbitrarily choose a date as the division point between two eras. But in reality one such age blends into another so slowly and so imperceptibly that no change is recognizable at the time. Only from the perspective of history can we look back and set an approximate date, perhaps within a century or two, as to when one era ceased and another began. So it is with the coming of the millennium. Undoubtedly it will follow the law of all the other great periods in the history of the church, being gradual and uncertain in its approach.

Principles of Interpretation

It is clear that each of the millennial views has been and is held by men whose sincerity and loyalty to the evangelical faith cannot be doubted. That believing Christians through the ages, using the same Bible and acknowledging it to be authoritative, have arrived at quite different conclusions appears to be due primarily to different methods of interpretation. Premillennialists place strong emphasis on literal interpretation and pride themselves on taking Scripture just as it is written. Post- and amillennialists on the other hand, mindful that much of both the Old and New Testaments is unquestionably given in figurative or symbolical language, have no objection on principle to figurative interpretation and readily accept that if the evidence indicates it is preferable. This causes premillennialists to charge that post- and amillennialists explain away or reject parts of the Bible. One premillennial writer says,

> Premillenarians . . . insist that one general rule of interpretation should be applied to all areas of theology and that prophecy does not require spiritualization any more than other aspects of truth. . . . History is history, not allegory. Facts are facts. Prophesied future events are just what they are prophesied.[4]

This general principle of interpretation has been expressed as "literal wherever possible" (H. Bonar) or "literal unless absurd" (Govett). One does not have to read far in the Bible to discover that not everything can be taken literally. Jesse F. Silver refers to "certain places" where some "other meaning" is designated. But he gives no rule by which those certain places are to be recognized. We find no labels in the Scripture itself telling us, "Take this literally," or "Take that figuratively." Evidently the individual reader must use his own judgment, backed by as much experience and common sense as he can muster. And that, of course, will vary endlessly from individual to individual.

As an example of what he means by literal interpretation Silver says, "Every prophecy pointing to the first advent of Christ was literally fulfilled to the letter in every detail." That statement has been made in substance by various other premillennialists. But it simply is not so. The very first Messianic prophecy in Scripture is found in Genesis 3:15, where, in pronouncing the curse upon the serpent God said, "He shall bruise your head, and you shall bruise his heel." Now that prophecy certainly was not fulfilled literally by a man crushing the head of a snake or by a snake biting the heel of a man. Rather it was fulfilled in a highly figurative sense when Christ gained a complete victory and triumphed over the devil and all his forces of evil at the cross. The last prophecy in the Old Testament is found in Malachi 4:5 and reads as follows, "Behold, I will send you Elijah the prophet before the great and terrible day of the LORD comes." That prophecy likewise was not fulfilled literally. Christ himself said that it was fulfilled in the person of John the Baptist (Mt. 11:14) who came in the spirit and power of Elijah.

Again, we have the prophecy of Isaiah:

A voice cries:

"In the wilderness prepare the way of the LORD,
    make straight in the desert a highway for our God.
Every valley shall be lifted up,
    and every mountain and hill be made low;
the uneven ground shall become level,
    and the rough places a plain.
And the glory of the LORD shall be revealed,
    and all flesh shall see it together,
    for the mouth of the LORD has spoken." (Is. 40:3-5)

This certainly was not fulfilled by a highway-building program in Palestine but rather in the work of John the Baptist who prepared the way for the public ministry of Jesus. John himself said, "For this is he who was spoken of by the prophet

Isaiah when he said, . . ." and then proceeded to quote these verses (Mt. 3:1-3; see also Lk. 3:3-6).

The words of Isaiah 9:1-2 regarding the people of Zebulun and Naphtali ("The people who walked in darkness have seen a great light; those who dwelt in the land of deep darkness, on them has light shined") are fulfilled figuratively in the ministry of Jesus. For Matthew says:

Now when he heard that John had been arrested, he withdrew into Galilee; and leaving Nazareth he went and dwelt in Capernaum by the sea, in the territory of Zebulun and Naphtali, that what was spoken by the prophet Isaiah might be fulfilled:

"The land of Zebulun and the land of Naphtali,
toward the sea, across the Jordan,
Galilee of the Gentiles—
the people who sat in darkness
have seen a great light,
and for those who sat in the region and shadow of death
light has dawned." (Mt. 4:12-16)

In these words Isaiah clearly was speaking of the spiritual darkness that exists wherever sin rules and of the spiritual light that would be brought to those lands when the Messiah came.

Many other Old Testament prophecies in figurative language might be cited, but surely these are sufficient to show that it simply is not true that "every prophecy pointing to the first advent of Christ was literally fulfilled to the letter in every detail."

That a great deal of the Bible is given in figurative or symbolic language, which by no stretch of the imagination can be taken literally, should be apparent to every one. We spiritualize these statements because we regard this as the only way in which their true meaning can be brought out. To cite only a few examples, in the midst of a very prosaic historical account of the deliverance of the children of Israel from Egypt, the providential and protective power of God is set forth in the words, "You have seen what I did to the Egyptians, and how I bore you on eagles' wings and brought you to myself" (Ex. 19:4). Palestine is described as "a land flowing with milk and honey" (Ex. 3:8). Read the twenty-third or ninety-first Psalm and note the almost continuous use of figurative language.

To spiritualize certain prophecies or other statements does not mean that we explain them away. Sometimes their true meaning is to be found only in the unseen spiritual world. Premillennialists often materialize and literalize the prophecies to such an extent that they keep them on an earthly level and miss their true and deeper meaning. That is exactly what the Jews did in their interpretation of Messianic prophecy. They looked for literal fulfillments with an earthly kingdom and a political ruler. The result was that they missed the redemptive element completely. When the Messiah came, they did not recognize him but instead rejected and crucified him. The fearful consequences of literalistic interpretation as it related to the first coming should put us on guard against making the same mistake concerning the Second Coming.

It is admittedly difficult in many instances to determine whether statements in Scripture should be taken literally or figuratively. As regards prophecy, that often cannot be determined until after the fulfillment. Most of the Bible, however, particularly the historical and the more didactic portions, clearly is to be understood literally, although some figurative expressions are found in these. But it is also clearly evident that many other portions must be understood figuratively. Even the premillennialists must take many expressions figuratively, or they become nonsense. Since the Bible gives no hard and fast rule for determining what is literal and what is figurative, we must study the nature of the material, the historical setting, the style and purpose of the writer, and then fall back on what for lack of a better term we may call "sanctified common sense." Naturally the conclusions will vary somewhat from individual to individual for we do not all think alike nor see alike.

It should hardly be necessary to point out that true post-millennialism is supernaturalistic through and through. Pre- and amillennialists sometimes represent this system as though it taught the conversion of the world through a merely humanistic and evolutionary process. Present day modernism does set forth a program of world betterment by natural rather than supernatural means, and opponents sometimes represent that as postmillennialism. But by no stretch of the imagination does such a system have any moral right to be called postmillennialism. That is not the sense in which the term has been used historically. Yet comments of that kind have given rise to much unjust criticism. Representative post-millennial theologians, such as Augustine, Brown, Hodge, Dabney and Warfield, have been consistent supernaturalists, and have believed in a fully inspired and authoritative Bible, and in the regenerating work of the Holy Spirit as the only means by which an individual can be brought to salvation.

On the other hand the distinguishing feature of present day modernism is its more or less consistent denial of the supernatural, that is, denial of the plenary inspiration of the Scriptures, the Trinity, the deity of Christ, blood atonement, miracles, final judgment, heaven and hell. It is concerned primarily with this life, and it proposes to reform the world through education, social and economic progress, improved health programs, better relations between capital and labor, and so on. Those things are good as far as they go and, wherever possible, should be encouraged. But they are only the by-products of true Christianity.

The fact that different views concerning the Second Coming of Christ and the millennium have been held and are held should not discourage anyone from making an earnest search for the truth. This situation in the field of theology is no different from that in the field of medicine, in which eminent doctors hold differing views on how certain diseases should be treated or how the human body should be cared for. We have, for instance, medical doctors, chiropractors, osteopaths, surgeons, dietetic specialists, physical exercise enthusiasts and so on. But that does not prevent us from believing in health nor from seeking the best methods to preserve health; nor does it save us from suffering the consequences if we choose wrongly.

The situation in politics and statesmanship is no different. We have various political parties, Republican, Democrat, Socialist, Labor, Communist and more, each advocating different principles for how the nation should be governed. We hear very conflicting opinions particularly at election time. There are various theories of education and of church government. In each of these spheres it is our duty to search diligently for the truth and so far as possible to separate truth from error. Our beliefs concerning the manner and time of the Second Coming of Christ will not change that event by one iota, but what we believe concerning those matters will very definitely affect our lives and conduct while we are waiting for that event.

It is to be regretted that these differences of opinion even among those who accept the Bible as the inspired and authoritative Word of God cannot always be dealt with by unprejudiced exegesis and friendly discussion rather than made the basis for quarrels or tests of orthodoxy. As a general rule premillennialists, basing their views on a more literal interpretation of Scripture, have a tendency to feel that those who do not accept their system hold a lower view of Scripture and that they are not consistently Christian. One might easily receive the impression from reading premillennial literature that only they believe fully in the Lord's return. It has even reached such a state in some dispensational circles that if one questions the personal reign of Christ in an earthly kingdom he is met with a question such as, "Then you do not believe that Christ is to return?" An examination of Bible institute catalogs reveals that most of them restrict faculty members to the premillennial view. Some are reluctant to graduate a student, or at least will give him a lower grade, if he does not accept that view. Prophetic conference literature presents a one-sided futurism and encourages the inference that opposing views are not evangelical. Some make a hobby of premillennialism, finding it with remarkable ingenuity in almost every prophecy and vision and promise from Genesis to Revelation, and giving it undue prominence in their preaching. Gray places the number of New Testament references to the coming of Christ at a minimum of three hundred, and Morgan says that on an average one verse in each twenty-five in the New Testament refers to it.

The differences between post-, a- and premillennialists, which should be treated as comparative nonessentials, actually divide the churches and become a serious impediment to Christian fellowship. Unquestionably the vagaries of dispensational extremists (not merely in such sects as Jehovah's Witnesses, Millennial Dawnists and some Pentecostal and Holiness groups, but also in the conventional evangelical churches) have divided Christians into antagonistic groups and have done much harm to the cause of Christianity.

In discussing these problems, then, two important facts should be kept in mind: (1) Evangelical post-, a- and premillennialists agree that the Bible is the Word of God, fully inspired and authoritative. They differ not in regard to the nature of Scripture authority but in regard to what they understand Scripture to teach. And (2) the three systems agree that there was a First Advent and that there will be a Second Advent, which will be personal, visible, glorious and as objective as was the Ascension from the Mount of Olives.

It should be added that the church has debated and reached conclusions and has embodied these conclusions in her creeds as the other great doctrines of the faith. But the subject of eschatology still remains in dispute. The manner of Christ's return and the kind of kingdom that he is setting up or will set up in this world is not agreed upon. For this reason the church in practically all of her branches has refused to make any one of the millennial interpretations an article of the creed and has preferred rather to accept as Christian brethren all those who believe in the fact of Christ's coming. Hence, while personally we may have very definite views concerning the manner and time of his coming, it would seem that our motto should be, "In essentials, unity; in nonessentials, liberty; in all things, charity."

AN HISTORIC PREMILLENNIAL RESPONSE
GEORGE ELDON LADD

There is so little appeal to Scripture that I have little to criticize. The argument that the world is getting better is a two-edged sword. One can equally well argue from empirical observation that the world is getting worse. In New Testament times, civilization enjoyed the great Pax Romana—two centuries when the Mediterranean world was at peace. This has never been repeated. Our lifetime has seen two worldwide wars and an unending series of lesser wars—in Korea, Vietnam, the Near East, Ireland, Lebanon. We have witnessed the rise of Nazism with its slaughter of six million Jews, the rise and fall of fascism, the rise and stabilization of Communist governments. The world today is literally an armed camp.

Boettner makes the mistake of defining premillennialism in terms of dispensationalism. As my chapter shows, I do not pursue the literalistic hermeneutic attributed to "premillennialists" by Boettner.

A DISPENSATIONAL
PREMILLENNIAL
RESPONSE
HERMAN A. HOYT

Without intending to demean the man who presents the post-millennial view, I must confess that this presentation leaves me in a sort of intellectual suspension. On the one hand I am unable to see any comparable relation of the doctrine to the world of reality round about me, and on the other I am unable to relate the doctrine to the substantial statements of the Scripture.

That there is a sense in which the kingdom of God is now being extended in the hearts of men by the preaching of the gospel, I would not question. I am strongly persuaded that God is today selecting a spiritual aristocracy for a future kingdom. And if that is what Boettner is saying in his introduction, I understand him. But for this to mean that the entire world will eventually be Christianized seems contrary to the facts of Scripture and experience. Surely this does not mean that the church is ushering in the millennium and that the millennium thus ushered in will be the world to which Christ returns. So far as I am able to see, no general resurrection or general judgment will immediately follow Christ's return.

Boettner hastens to define postmillennialism as an expectation of a golden age of spiritual prosperity during this present dispensation of the church, a prosperity brought about by forces now active in the world. This period is much longer than a thousand years, he says, indicating that any literal adherence to the words of Scripture is not regarded as essential in this doctrine. But even though he emphasizes the fact that the golden age is in the era of spiritual prosperity, he also insists that this is reflected in "an uplifted social, economic, political and cultural life of mankind" (p. 117). When this change is experienced the world at large will enjoy a state of righteousness now realized in very small groups and isolated areas.

This must mean that this millennial kingdom is yet future. Perhaps it is in order to ask when or at what stage we can be sure this kingdom is actually realized. Boettner insists this does not mean there will ever be a time when everyone will be a Christian or when all sin will be abolished. But he does think that evil in all its many forms will eventually be reduced to negligible proportions and that Christian principles will be the rule and not the exception. It is then that Christ will return. But does this square with the Scriptures? Or do we see any evidence now?

He is undoubtedly right that the great commission was intended to urge universal proclamation of the gospel (Mt. 28: 18-20). This included effectual evangelization in the sense of making disciples of all nations. But he does admit the church has been extremely negligent during the past nineteen centuries. The gospel is not at fault, but certainly there is amazing failure on the part of the church to carry forward its responsibility. Is there any reason to believe that the situation is moving ahead? Or is it possible that the spiritual situation is in decline? Nevertheless Boettner, like those who hold differing views, looks for "the blessed hope and appearing of the glory of the great God and our Savior Jesus Christ" (Tit. 2:13, ASV).

Inadequate terminology does constitute difficulty in presenting the various views. The millennium which the post-millennialist looks for is quite different from that expected by the premillennialist. This difference involves not only time and manner of appearance but also nature and control. As viewed by the postmillennialist, the golden age will not be essentially different from the age in which we now live, except in degree. As increasing numbers of people are converted to Christianity there will be a gradual merging of the present age into the millennial state. This is the progressive realization of a spiritual kingdom in the hearts of men. Obviously this stands in bold contrast to the millennium envisioned by the premillennialist and seems to ignore the clear statements of Scripture concerning the growing sinfulness of the world and the necessity for divine action to establish the kingdom (Mt. 13: 24-30, 36-43).

Boettner is right in holding to the conviction that through the provision of redemption a greater part of the human race will be saved. He thinks that the position held by premillennialists, at least some of them, is that the greater part will be lost. But that is only true as far as the present age is concerned. In the period of tribulation and millennium, the greatest period of evangelization in the history of the world will take place—during the tribulation under the most adverse conditions and during the millennium under the most favorable. Because he does not hold a premillennial position, he has used Scriptures that the premillennialist feels belong to the tribulation and the millennium to support his position (Zech. 9:10; Rev. 7:9-10).

There is a sense in which the world is growing better, as Boettner affirms. But there is also a sense in which the age is growing worse. These trends must be carefully measured in the light of Scripture. All progress, including moral and spiritual progress, should be reason for hope in a coming millennium here on the earth ushered in by the Lord Jesus Christ.

But the spiritual decline is reason for warning of an approaching end of the age with judgment from Christ. This decline is coming in spite of the spiritual influence of the church and suggests that real hope must be vested in the personal appearing of the Lord Jesus Christ. This is not to ignore international good will, the translation and dissemination of Scriptures, the worldwide missionary movements, the increasing Christian population and the many other factors contributing to a better society. But in assessing these values, one dare not shut his eyes to the trends that point to the disintegration and demoralization of society in preparation for the end of the age.

Boettner concludes his treatise with a discussion of principles of interpretation. As with other writers, he readily concedes here that the issues center at this point. As expected, he must defend spiritualization in order to support his position. And in doing this, he must deny literalism in the interpretation of Scripture. After citing a statement by Silver contending that prophecies of Christ's first coming were literally fulfilled, he seeks to destroy Silver's statement by looking at the first prophecy concerning Christ's coming—Gen. 3:15. "He shall bruise your head, and you shall bruise his heel." He insists that this prophecy was not literally fulfilled in the sense of a man crushing the head of a snake or a snake biting the heel of a man. And he is right, if that is what is meant by literalism. But that is not what is meant. When a passage uses a figure of speech, it is the literal interpretation to discover the meaning of the figure in the Scripture and take it at its face value. In this case the serpent is clearly defined as the devil. And the biting of the heel is the temporary impairment of Christ in the fulfillment of his ministry. The same principle is to be applied to other passages that employ figures of speech.

When citing a prophecy from Malachi 4:5 and the New Testament reference to it, Boettner erred in ignoring part of the text in Matthew (11:14). Christ said that John the Baptist would have stood for Elijah if they would receive him. But they did not which must mean that Elijah is yet to come. The reason Christ could make reference to John the Baptist as he did was that John the Baptist came in the spirit and power of Elijah (Lk. 1:17).It therefore seems obvious that there was a principle in relation to Elijah which was also true of John the Baptist, and the reference made by Christ was by way of application and not interpretation. Therefore the effort to disprove the principle of literal interpretation fails when using this text for it is not interpretation that is under consideration.

No dispensationalist disputes the fact that many figures of speech are used in the Scriptures. He does insist that it is literal to interpret those figures as the immediate or more remote context of the Bible requires. But it is also true that there are many passages from the Old Testament that are applied by the New Testament because there is some principle in common with the issue at hand. This is not interpretation, and therefore care should be taken not to draw false inferences.

I have many volumes in my library from the pen of Dr. Boettner, and I count them of high value. I believe that this man is a child of God and has a real hope for the coming of Christ. This does not mean that he is necessarily right in the system of postmillennialism which he endorses. It could mean that he is wrong and has shut himself out from vistas of blessing for failing to endorse a correct system of interpretation. Because eschatological views have overtones that affect other areas of theology, the various views in this area cannot be treated as trifling matters. This does not mean that some charity may not be extended toward those who espouse opposing views. Though I have deep feelings concerning the implications of eschatology, I do hold this brother in high esteem.

AN AMILLENNIAL RESPONSE
ANTHONY A. HOEKEMA

There is much in Boettner's chapter with which I agree. Among the points of agreement are the following: First, the kingdom of God is now being extended in the world through the preaching of the gospel and the saving work of the Holy Spirit in the hearts of men (p. 117). Second, Christ will return visibly and in great glory; at his coming he will raise the dead, execute judgment and usher in the final state (pp. 119-20). Third, not all biblical prophecy is to be interpreted literally, but room must be left for both literal and figurative interpretations (pp. 134-38). And last, the millennium is an indefinitely long period of time, perhaps much longer than a literal thousand years (p. 117).

I disagree with this author, however, on the question of how we must conceive of the millennium. On page 117 Boettner tells us, "The millennium to which the postmillennialist looks forward is thus a golden age of spiritual prosperity during this present dispensation, that is, during the Church Age. This is to be brought about through forces now active in the world." He goes on to say that this future golden age is to be introduced gradually, as the gospel is preached more and more widely and as a growing proportion of the world's inhabitants are converted to Christianity. Sin will then not be eliminated but will be reduced to a minimum, and Christian principles of belief and conduct will become the accepted standards. The millennium will be brought to an end by the Second Coming of Christ, the resurrection and the final judgment (p. 121).

What makes Boettner's essay difficult to reply to is that he nowhere gives us his interpretation of Revelation 20:1-6—the only biblical passage which speaks of a millennium. One would certainly expect that an evangelical scholar who embraces the postmillennial view while holding to the inspiration and normativity of the Bible would give us an exegetical study of this passage, to show that his view of the millennium grows directly out of that study. But one looks in vain for such a study.

In the absence of this, all we can do is to assume that Boettner believes that the millennial golden age which he expects is taught in Revelation 20:1-6. If this assumption is correct, I would counter that Revelation 20:4-6 does not refer to a ruling with Christ of believers who are still on earth and have not yet died, but rather to a ruling with Christ of the souls of believers who have died. The very phrase "the rest of the dead" in verse 5 indicates that this vision does not concern believers who are still living but believers who have already died. If, however, Boettner would agree that Revelation 20:4-6 does not describe a millennial reign on earth but a reign of the souls of deceased believers during the intermediate state (as he indeed says in his book, *The Millennium*, p. 66), then on what scriptural grounds does he base his expectation of a future millennial golden age on earth?

Actually, Boettner gives only two main arguments for his position. The first of these arguments, developed on pages 123-25, is that the number of the saved will far exceed the number of the lost. One may not be fully convinced of this claim by the passages the author adduces. But even if one should be inclined to agree that the number of the saved will greatly exceed the number of the lost, how would this prove that there will be an earthly millennial golden age?

Boettner's second argument is that the world is growing better (pp. 125-33). Many readers will be inclined to take issue with the author on this point. To begin with, his sketch of world conditions is seriously out of date. Little or nothing is said, for example, about the war in Vietnam, the tension in the Middle East, the ecological crisis, the world food shortage or the energy crisis. Surely the world picture today is much different from what it was in 1957! Besides, the author seems to pick out only the favorable aspects of world conditions while ignoring unfavorable aspects. He mentions, for example, how much progress has been made in the areas of transportation and communication. But certainly modern inventions are used for purposes which are evil as well as good! Is it not far more realistic to say that as the kingdom of God advances in this world there is a corresponding advance of the kingdom of evil?

But once again, even if one should agree with Boettner that the world is indeed getting better, how would this prove that the world is moving on toward a millennial golden age? Is it not conceivable that there may be an abrupt shift in the fortunes of mankind? What certainty do we have that the age in which we now live will not be followed by a new Dark Age?

In this connection it is disconcerting to find no reference in Boettner's essay to biblical teachings about the apostasy (or "falling away"), the great tribulation or the revelation of the Antichrist. Nor is any comment made about Jesus' words recorded in Luke 18:8, "When the Son of man comes, will he find faith on earth?" Those words suggest that at the time of Christ's return the number of true believers may indeed be very small and do not seem to support Boettner's contention that "before Christ comes again we shall see a Christianized world" (p. 125).

I conclude that Boettner's view of the millennium, attractive though it is, is not solidly based on Scripture.

IV

AMILLENNIALISM

AMILLENNIALISM
ANTHONY A. HOEKEMA

My discussion of the amillennial understanding of the millennium will include the following topics: the interpretation of the book of Revelation, the interpretation of Revelation 20:1-6, a look at two Old Testament passages commonly viewed as predicting an earthly millennial kingdom, a brief sketch of amillennial eschatology and a summarizing statement of some of the implications of amillennial eschatology.

A word should first be said about terminology. The term *amillennialism* is not a happy one. It suggests that amillennialists either do not believe in any millennium or that they simply ignore the first six verses of Revelation 20, which speak of a millennial reign. Neither of these two statements is true. Though it is true that amillennialists do not believe in a literal thousand-year earthly reign which will follow the return of Christ, the term *amillennialism* is not an accurate description of their view. Professor Jay E. Adams of Westminster Seminary in Philadelphia has suggested that the term *amillennialism* be replaced by the expression *realized millennialism*.[1] The latter term, to be sure, describes the "amillennial" position more accurately than the usual term, since "amillennialists" believe that the millennium of Revelation 20 is not exclusively future but is now in process of realization. The expression *realized millennialism*, however, is a rather clumsy one, replacing a simple prefix with a three-syllable word. Despite the disadvantages and limitations of the word, therefore, I shall continue to use the shorter and more common term, *amillennialism.*

The Interpretation of the Book of Revelation
To see the background for the amillennial view of the millennium, we should first of all concern ourselves with the question of the interpretation of the book of Revelation. Let us assume, for example, that the book of Revelation is to be interpreted in an exclusively futuristic sense, referring only to events that are to happen around or at the time of Christ's Second Coming. Let us further assume that what is presented in Revelation 20 must necessarily follow, in chronological order, what was described in chapter 19. We are then virtually compelled to believe that the thousand-year reign depicted in 20:4 must come after the return of Christ described in 19:11. But if we see Revelation 20:1-6 as describing what takes place during the entire history of the church, beginning with the first coming of Christ, we will have an understanding of the millennium of Revelation 20 which is quite different from the one just mentioned. For this reason it will be necessary first to say something about the way in which the book of Revelation should be interpreted.

The system of interpretation of the book of Revelation which seems most satisfactory to me (though it is not without its difficulties) is that known as *progressive parallelism*, ably defended by William Hendriksen in *More Than Conquerors*, his commentary on Revelation.[2] According to this view, the book of Revelation consists of seven sections which run parallel to each other, each of which depicts the church and the world from the time of Christ's first coming to the time of his second. The first of these seven sections is found in chapters 1—3. John sees the risen and glorified Christ walking in the midst of seven golden lampstands. In obedience to Christ's command John now proceeds to write letters to each of the seven churches of Asia Minor. The vision of the glorified Christ together with the letters to the seven churches obviously form a unit. As we read these letters we are impressed with two things. First, there are references to events, people and places of the time when the book of Revelation was written. Second, the principles, commendations and warnings contained in these letters have value for the church of all time. These two observations, in fact, provide a clue for the interpretation of the entire book. Since the book of Revelation was addressed to the church of the first century A.D., its message had reference to events occurring at that time and was therefore meaningful for the Christians of that day. But since the book was also intended for the church through the ages, its message is still relevant for us today.

The second of these seven sections is the vision of the seven seals found in chapters 4—7. John is caught up to heaven and sees God sitting on his radiant throne. He then sees the Lamb that had been slain taking the scroll sealed with seven seals from the hand of the one who was sitting on the throne. The various seals are broken, and various divine judgments on the world are described. In this vision we see the church suffering trial and persecution against the background of the victory of Christ.

The third section, found in chapters 8—11, describes the seven trumpets of judgment. In this vision we see the church avenged, protected and victorious.

The fourth section, chapters 12—14, begins with the vision of the woman giving birth to a son while the dragon waits to devour him as soon as he is born—an obvious reference to the birth of Christ. The rest of the section describes the continued opposition of the dragon (who stands for Satan) to the church. This section also introduces us to the two beasts who are the dragon's helpers: the beast out of the sea and the beast out of the earth.

The fifth section is found in chapters 15—16. It describes the seven bowls of wrath, thus depicting in a very graphic way the final visitation of God's wrath on those who remain impenitent.

The sixth section, chapters 17—19, describes the fall of Babylon and of the beasts. Babylon stands for the worldly city —the forces of secularism and godlessness which are in opposition to the kingdom of God. The end of chapter 19 depicts the fall and final punishment of the dragon's two helpers: the beast out of the sea, and the false prophet, who appears to be identified with the beast out of the earth (see 16:13).

The seventh section, chapters 20—22, narrates the doom of the dragon, thus completing the description of the overthrow of the enemies of Christ. In addition, it describes the final judgment, the final triumph of Christ and his church, and the renewed universe, here called the new heaven and the new earth.

Note that though these seven sections are parallel to each other, they also reveal a certain amount of eschatological progress. The last section, for example, takes us further into the future than the other sections. Although the final judgment has already been announced in 1:7 and has been briefly described in 6:12-17, it is not set forth in full detail until we come to 20:11-15. Though the final joy of the redeemed in the life to come has been hinted at in 7:15-17, it is not until we reach chapter 21 that we find a detailed and elaborate description of the blessedness of life on the new earth (21:1—22:5). Hence this method of interpretation is called *progressive* parallelism.

There is eschatological progression in these seven sections, not only regarding the individual sections but also regarding the book as a whole. If we grant that the book of Revelation depicts the struggle between Christ and his church on the one hand and the enemies of Christ and the church on the other, we may say that the first half of the book (chapters 1—11) describes the struggle on earth, picturing the church as it is persecuted by the world. The second half of the book, however (chapters 12—22), gives us the deeper spiritual background of this struggle, describing the persecution of the church by the dragon (Satan) and his helpers. In the light of this analysis we see how the last section of the book (chapters 20—22) falls into place. This last section describes the judgment which falls on Satan, and his final doom. Since Satan is the supreme opponent of Christ, it stands to reason that his doom should be narrated last.

The Interpretation of Revelation 20:1-6

We are now ready to proceed to the interpretation of Revelation 20:1-6, the only passage in the Bible which speaks explicitly of a thousand-year reign. Note first that the passage obviously divides itself into two parts: verses 1-3, which describe the binding of Satan; and verses 4-6, which describe the thousand-year reign of souls with Christ.

The premillennial interpretation of these verses sees them as describing a millennial reign of Christ on earth which will occur after his Second Coming. And it is true that the Second Coming of Christ has been referred to in the previous chapter (see 19:11-16). If, then, one thinks of Revelation 20 as describing what follows chronologically after what is described in chapter 19, one would indeed conclude that the millennium of Revelation 20:1-6 will come after the return of Christ.

As has been indicated above, however, chapters 20—22 comprise the last of the seven sections of the book of Revelation and therefore do not describe what follows the return of Christ. Rather, Revelation 20:1 takes us back once again to the beginning of the New Testament era.

That this is the proper interpretation of these verses is clear not only from what has been developed above, but also from the fact that this chapter describes the defeat and final doom of Satan. Surely the defeat of Satan began with the first coming of Christ, as has already been clearly spelled out in chapter 12:7-9. That the millennial reign described in verses 4-6 occurs before the Second Coming of Christ is evident from the fact that the final judgment, described in verses 11-15 of this chapter, is pictured as coming after the thousand-year reign. Not only in the book of Revelation but elsewhere in the New Testament the final judgment is associated with the Second Coming of Christ. (See Revelation 22:12 and the following passages: Mt. 16:27; 25:31-32; Jude 14-15; and especially 2 Thess. 1:7-10.) This being the case, it is obvious that the thousand-year reign of Revelation 20:4-6 must occur *before* and *not after* the Second Coming of Christ.

Let us now look closely at Revelation 20:1-6 itself. We begin with verses 1-3, reproduced here from the New International Version:

> And I saw an angel coming down out of heaven, having the key to the Abyss and holding in his hand a great chain. He seized the dragon, that ancient serpent, who is the devil, or Satan, and bound him for a thousand years. He threw him into the Abyss, and locked and sealed it over him, to keep him from deceiving the nations any more until the thousand years were ended. After that, he must be set free for a short time.

In these verses we have a description of the binding of Satan. The dragon, here clearly identified as "the devil, or Satan," is said to be bound for a thousand years and then cast into a place called "the Abyss." The purpose of this binding is "to keep him from deceiving the nations any more until the thousand years were ended."

The book of Revelation is full of symbolic numbers. Obviously the number "thousand" which is used here must not be interpreted in a literal sense. Since the number ten signifies completeness, and since a thousand is ten to the third power, we may think of the expression "a thousand years" as standing for a complete period, a very long period of indeterminate length. In agreement with what was said above about the structure of the book and in the light of verses 7-15 of this very chapter (which describe Satan's "little season," the final battle and the final judgment), we may conclude that this thousand-year period extends from Christ's first coming to just before his Second Coming.

Since the "lake of fire" mentioned in verses 10, 14 and 15 is obviously a description of the place of final punishment, the "Abyss" mentioned in verses 1 and 3 must not be the place of final punishment. The word *Abyss* should rather be thought of as a figurative description of the way in which Satan's activities will be curbed during the thousand-year period.

What is meant, then, by the binding of Satan? In Old Testament times, at least in the post-Abrahamic era, all the nations of the world except Israel were, so to speak, under Satan's rule. At that time the people of Israel were the recipients of God's special revelation, so that they knew God's truth about themselves, about their sinfulness, and about the way they could obtain forgiveness and salvation. During this same time, however, the other nations of the world did not know that truth, and were therefore in ignorance and error (see Acts 17:30)—except for an occasional person, family or city which came into contact with God's special revelation. One could say that during this time these nations were deceived by Satan, as our first parents had been deceived by Satan when they fell into sin in the Garden of Eden.

Just before his ascension, however, Christ gave his disciples his Great Commission: "Go and make disciples of all nations" (Mt. 28:19, NIV). At this point one can well imagine the disciples raising a disturbing question: How can we possibly do this if Satan continues to deceive the nations the way he has in the past? In Revelation 20:1-3 John gives a reassuring answer to this question. Paraphrased, his answer goes something like this: "During the gospel era which has now been ushered in, Satan will not be able to continue deceiving the nations the way he did in the past, for he has been bound. During this entire period, therefore, you, Christ's disciples, will be able to preach the gospel and make disciples of all nations."

This does not imply that Satan can do no harm whatever while he is bound. It means only what John says here: While Satan is bound he cannot deceive the nations in such a way as to keep them from learning about the truth of God. Later in the chapter we are told that when the thousand years are over, Satan will be released from his prison and will go out to deceive the nations of the world to gather them together to fight against and, if possible, to destroy the people of God (verses 7-9). This, however, he cannot do while he is bound. We conclude, then, that the binding of Satan during the gospel age means that, first, he cannot prevent the spread of the gospel, and second, he cannot gather all the enemies of Christ together to attack the church.

Is there any indication in the New Testament that Satan was bound at the time of the first coming of Christ? Indeed there is. When the Pharisees accused Jesus of casting out demons by the power of Satan, Jesus replied, "How can one enter a strong man's house and plunder his goods, unless he first binds the strong man?" (Mt. 12:29). Interestingly enough, the word used by Matthew to describe the binding of the strong man is the same word used in Revelation 20 to describe the binding of Satan. One could say that Jesus bound the devil when he triumphed over him in the wilderness, refusing to give in to his temptations. Jesus' casting out of demons, so he teaches us in this passage, was evidence of this triumph. One could counter that the binding of Satan mentioned here is reported in connection with the casting out of demons rather than in connection with the preaching of the gospel. But I would reply that the casting out of demons is an evidence of the presence of the kingdom of God (Mt. 12:28) and that it is precisely because the kingdom of God has come that the gospel can now be preached to all the nations (see Mt. 13:24-30, 47-50).

When the seventy returned from their preaching mission, they said to Jesus, "Lord, even the demons submit to us in your name." Jesus replied, "I saw Satan fall like lightning from heaven" (Lk. 10:17-18, NIV). These words, needless to say, must not be interpreted literally. They must rather be understood to mean that Jesus saw in the works his disciples were doing an indication that Satan's kingdom had just been dealt a crushing blow—that, in fact, a certain binding of Satan, a certain restriction of his power, had just taken place. In this instance Satan's fall or binding is associated directly with the missionary activity of Jesus' disciples.

Another passage which ties in the restriction of Satan's activities with Christ's missionary outreach is John 12:31-32: "Now is the time for judgment on this world; now the prince of this world will be driven out. But I, when I am lifted up from the earth, will draw all men to myself" (NIV). It is interesting to note that the verb here translated "driven out" (*ekballō*) is derived from the same root as the word used in Revelation 20:3, "He [the angel] threw [*ballō*] him [Satan] into the Abyss." Even more important, however, is the observation that Satan's being "driven out" or "cast out" (RSV) is here associated with the fact that not only Jews but men of all nationalities shall be drawn to Christ as he hangs on the cross.

We see then that the binding of Satan described in Revelation 20:1-3 means that throughout the gospel age in which we now live the influence of Satan, though certainly not annihilated, is so curtailed that he cannot prevent the spread of the gospel to the nations of the world. Because of the binding of Satan during this present age, the nations cannot conquer the church, but the church is conquering the nations.[3]

We go on now to verses 4-6, the passage dealing with the thousand-year reign. In the New International Version, these verses read,

> I saw thrones on which were seated those who had been given authority to judge. And I saw the souls of those who had been beheaded because of their testimony for Jesus and because of the word of God. They had not worshiped the beast or his image and had not received his mark on their foreheads or their hands. They came to life and reigned with Christ a thousand years. (The rest of the dead did not come to life until the thousand years were ended.) This is the first resurrection. Blessed and holy are those who have part in the first resurrection. The second death has no power over them, but they will be priests of God and of Christ and will reign with him for a thousand years.

We noted previously that verses 1-3 speak of a "thousand-year" period. We now observe that verses 4-6 also refer to a period of a thousand years. Though it is possible to understand the "thousand years" of verses 4-6 as describing a period of time different from the "thousand years" of verses 1-3, there is no compelling reason why we should do so. We may therefore safely assume that verses 1-3 and verses 4-6 concern the same "thousand-year" period. That period, as we saw, spans the entire New Testament dispensation, from the time of the first coming of Christ to just before the time of Christ's Second Coming.

Let us now take a closer look at verse 4: "I saw thrones on which were seated those who had been given authority to judge." The first question we must face here is, Where are these thrones? Leon Morris points out that in the book of Revelation the word "throne" is used forty-seven times and that all but three of these thrones (2:13; 13:2; 16:10) appear to be in heaven.[4] When we add to this consideration the fact that John sees "the souls of those who had been beheaded," we are confirmed in the conclusion that the locale of John's vision has now shifted to heaven. We may say then that whereas the thousand-year period described in these six verses is the same throughout, verses 1-3 describe what happens on earth during this time, and verses 4-6 depict what happens in heaven.

John sees those who had been given authority to judge (literally, those to whom judgment had been given) sitting on thrones. The book of Revelation is much concerned about matters of justice, particularly for persecuted Christians. It is therefore highly significant that in John's vision those sitting on thrones are given authority to judge. John's description of them as "sitting on thrones" is a concrete way of expressing the thought that they are reigning with Christ (see the last part of v. 4). Apparently this reigning includes the authority to make judgments. Whether this means simply agreeing with and being thankful for the judgments made by Christ, or whether it means that those sitting on the thrones are given the opportunity to make their own judgments about earthly matters, we are not told. In any event the reigning with Christ described here apparently includes having some part in Christ's judging activity (see Dan. 7:22).

We ask next, Who are seated on these thrones? The answer is given in the rest of the verse: "And I saw the souls of those who had been beheaded because of their testimony for Jesus and because of the word of God." Since John tells us that he saw "the souls of those who had been beheaded," it is quite clear that he is not talking about people who are still living on the earth. Sometimes, to be sure, the word here rendered "souls," *psuchai,* may be used to describe people who are still living on the earth—as, for example, in Acts 2:41: "And there were added that day about three thousand souls." But in Revelation 20:4 this meaning of the word *psuchai* will not work. One cannot translate *tas psuchas tōn pepelekismenōn* as "the people of those who had been beheaded," or as "the men of those who had been beheaded." Here the word *psuchai* must denote the souls of people who had died. This text is, in fact, a kind of parallel to an earlier passage in Revelation 6:9: "When he opened the fifth seal, I saw under the altar the souls of those who had been slain because of the word of God and the testimony they had maintained."

If one should ask how John could see the souls of those who had died, the answer is, John saw all this in a vision. One could just as well ask, How could John see an angel laying hold of the devil and binding him for a thousand years?

John sees the souls of those who had been beheaded because of their testimony for Jesus and because of the word of God. In other words, he sees the souls of the martyrs—believers who had suffered martyrs' deaths because of their faithfulness to Christ. When John wrote Revelation, many Christians were being martyred for their faith. Needless to say, the vision here recorded would bring great comfort to the relatives and friends of these martyrs: John sees their souls as now sitting on thrones in heaven, taking part in the work of judging.

"They had not worshiped the beast or his image and had not received his mark on their foreheads or their hands." The New International Version renders these words as if they were a further description of the martyrs referred to in the preceding clause. There is, however, another possibility—the possibility conveyed by the translation found in the American

Standard Version: "and such as worshiped not the beast, neither his image, and received not the mark upon their forehead and upon their hand." Earlier in the book unbelieving opponents of Christ and his kingdom were described as those who worship the beast or his image and who receive the mark of the beast on their foreheads or on their hands (see 13:8, 15-17; 14:9-11). Conversely, believers who remained faithful to their Lord are described as those who were victorious over the beast (15:2) or who did not worship the beast or his image (13:15). I take it, therefore, that in the clause we are now considering John is describing a wider group than just the martyrs. By "those who had not worshiped the beast or his image and had not received his mark" John means all Christians who had remained true to Christ and had resisted anti-Christian powers—all Christians, in other words, who had remained faithful to the end. Those who had died a martyr's death would constitute a part of this group but not the whole group. (Though John does not here specifically speak of "souls," we may safely assume that he is still talking about the souls of believers who have died, since he began by speaking about the souls of the martyrs who had been slain.)

Now follow the most controversial words in the passage: "They came to life and reigned with Christ a thousand years." Premillennial interpreters, whether dispensational or nondispensational, understand these words as referring to a literal resurrection from the dead, and therefore find in this passage proof for a thousand-year reign of Christ on earth, after his Second Coming. Is this the correct interpretation of the passage?

It must be granted that the Greek word rendered "came to life," *ezēsan,* can refer to a physical resurrection (see, for example, Mt. 9:18; Rom. 14:9; 2 Cor. 13:4; Rev. 2:8). The question is, however, whether this is what the word means here.

That John is speaking of a kind of resurrection here is apparent from the second sentence of verse 5: "This is the first resurrection"—words which obviously refer to the living and reigning with Christ of verse 4. But is this "first resurrection" a physical resurrection—a raising of the body from the dead? Obviously not, since the raising of the body from the dead is mentioned later in the chapter as something distinct from what is described here (see vv. 11-13). Only if one believes in two bodily resurrections—one of believers at the beginning of the millennium and another of unbelievers after the millennium—will one be able to understand the *ezēsan* of verse 4 as referring to a bodily resurrection. Since the Scriptures elsewhere clearly teach only one bodily resurrection which will include both believers and unbelievers (see Jn. 5:28-29; Acts 24:15), what is described in the last clause of verse 4 must be something other than the physical or bodily resurrection which is yet to come.

What is meant, then, by the words "they came to life and reigned with Christ a thousand years"? The clue has already been given in verse 4a. There John said, "I saw thrones on which were seated those who had been given authority to judge." The rest of the verse makes plain that those sitting on the thrones were the souls of people who had died—martyrs for the faith and other Christians who had remained true to Christ to the very end of their lives. This is the group which John sees as "living and reigning with Christ." Though these believers have died, John sees them as alive, not in the bodily sense, but in the sense that they are enjoying life in heaven in fellowship with Christ. This life is a life of great happiness (see Paul's words in Phil. 1:23 and 2 Cor. 5:8). It is a life in which they sit on thrones, sharing in the reign of Christ over all things, even sharing in his judging activity! This heavenly reigning is a fulfillment of a promise recorded earlier in the book: "To him who overcomes, I will give the right to sit with me on my throne, just as I overcame and sat down with my Father on his throne" (3:21, NIV).

We can appreciate the significance of this vision when we remember that in John's time the church was sorely oppressed and frequently persecuted. It would be of great comfort to those believers to know that though many of their fellow Christians had died, some even having been cruelly executed as martyrs, these deceased fellow believers were now actually alive in heaven as far as their souls were concerned—living and reigning with Christ. This living and reigning with Christ, John goes on to say, shall continue throughout the thousand years—that is, throughout the entire gospel era, until Christ shall come again to raise the bodies of these believers from the grave.

There is no indication in these verses that John is describing an earthly millennial reign. The scene, as we saw, is set in heaven. Nothing is said in verses 4-6 about the earth, about Palestine as the center of this reign or about the Jews.[5] The thousand-year reign of Revelation 20:4 is a reign with Christ in heaven of the souls of believers who have died. This reign is not something to be looked for in the future; it is going on now, and will be until Christ returns. Hence the term *realized millennialism* is an apt description of the view here defended— if it be remembered that the millennium in question is not an earthly but a heavenly one.

The next sentence, verse 5a, is of a parenthetical nature, and is therefore properly put between parentheses in the New International Version: "The rest of the dead did not come to life until the thousand years were ended." I have already given the reason why I do not believe that these words describe a bodily resurrection which is to take place after the millennium. The word *ezēsan* ("lived" or "came to life") as it is used in this sentence must mean the same thing that it meant in the preceding sentence. John is here speaking about the unbelieving dead—the "rest of the dead," in distinction from the believing dead whom he has just been describing. When he says that the rest of the dead did not live or come to life, he means the exact opposite of what he had just said about the believing dead. The unbelieving dead, he is saying, did not live or reign with Christ during this thousand-year period. Whereas believers after death enjoy a new kind of life in heaven with Christ in which they share in Christ's reign, unbelievers after death share nothing of either this life or this reign.

That this is true throughout the thousand-year period is indicated by the words, "until the thousand years were ended." The Greek word here translated "until," *achri*, means that what is said here held true during the entire length of the thousand-year period. The use of the word *until* does not imply that these unbelieving dead will live and reign with Christ after this period has ended. If this were the case, we would have expected a clear statement to this effect. (For an example of this kind of statement, see Rev. 20:3.) Rather, what happens to the unbelieving dead after the thousand years have ended is what is called in verse 6 "the second death." When it is said in verse 6 that the "second death" has no power over the believing dead, it is implied that the "second death" does have power over the unbelieving dead. What is meant by "the second death"? Verse 14 explains: "This is the second death, even the lake of fire" (ASV). The second death, then, means everlasting punishment after the resurrection of the body. As far as the unbelieving dead are concerned, therefore, there will be a change after the thousand years have ended, but it will be a change not for the better but for the worse.

Now John goes on to say, "This is the first resurrection." These words depict what has happened to the believing dead whom John was describing at the end of verse 4, previous to the parenthetical statement just discussed. In the light of what was said above, we must understand these words as describing not a bodily resurrection but rather the transition from physical death to life in heaven with Christ. This transition is here called a "resurrection"—an unusual use of the word, to be sure, but perfectly understandable against the background of the preceding context. The expression "the first resurrection" implies that there will indeed be a "second resurrection" for these believing dead—the resurrection of the body which will take place when Christ returns at the end of the thousand-year period.

John now says, in verse 6, "Blessed and holy are those who have part in the first resurrection." The next words give the reason for this blessedness: "The second death has no power over them." The second death, as we saw, means eternal punishment. These words about the second death imply that the "first resurrection" which John has just mentioned is not a bodily resurrection. For if believers should here be thought of as having been physically raised, with glorified bodies, they would already be enjoying the full and total bliss of the life to come, and it would not need to be said that over them the second death has no power.

"But they will be priests of God and of Christ and will reign with him for a thousand years" (v. 6b). During this entire thousand-year period, therefore, the believing dead shall worship God and Christ as priests and shall reign with Christ as kings. Though John is here thinking only about the thousand-year period which extends until Christ returns, the closing chapters of the book of Revelation indicate that after Christ's return and after the resurrection of the body these believing dead shall be able to worship God, serve God and reign with Christ in an even richer way than they are now doing. They shall then worship and serve God throughout all eternity in sinless perfection with glorified bodies on the new earth.

This, then, is the amillennial interpretation of Revelation

20:1-6. So understood, the passage says nothing about an earthly reign of Christ over a primarily Jewish kingdom. Rather, it describes the reigning with Christ in heaven of the souls of believers who have died. They reign during the time between their death and Christ's Second Coming.

The Interpretation of Old Testament Prophecy
There is a basic difference in the method of biblical interpretation employed by premillennialists and amillennialists. Premillennialists, particularly those of dispensationalist persuasion, are committed to what is commonly called the "literal" interpretation of Old Testament prophecy. John F. Walvoord, a prominent spokesman for the dispensational premillennial viewpoint, defines the hermeneutical method of this school of interpretation:

> The premillennial position is that the Bible should be interpreted in its ordinary grammatical and historical meaning in all areas of theology unless contextual or theological reasons make it clear that this was not intended by the writer.[6]

In his discussion of this principle Walvoord admits that sometimes an Old Testament passage contains indications that certain parts of it are not to be interpreted literally but figuratively—for example, the "rod of his mouth" with which Christ is said to smite the earth in Isaiah 11:4.[7]

Amillennialists, on the other hand, believe that though many Old Testament prophecies are indeed to be interpreted literally, many others are to be interpreted in a nonliteral way.[8] In the abstract, an amillennialist might agree with the definition of the premillennial hermeneutical method given by Walvoord. The difference between an amillennial and a premillennial interpreter comes out when each tries to indicate which prophecies must be interpreted literally and which prophecies are to be interpreted in a nonliteral sense. On this question there would be wide divergence of opinion.

There is no space in this short chapter to go into these differences of interpretation in depth. It will be helpful, however, for us to take a brief look at two Old Testament passages which are commonly understood by premillennialists as picturing a future earthly millennial reign. When we do so we shall see that the premillennial interpretation of these two representative passages is by no means the only possible one.

Let us look first of all at Isaiah 11:6-9 as rendered by the New Scofield Bible:

The wolf also shall dwell with the lamb, and the leopard shall lie down with the kid; and the calf and the young lion and the fatling together, and a little child shall lead them. And the cow and the bear shall feed; their young ones shall lie down together. And the lion shall eat straw like the ox. And the nursing child shall play on the hole of the asp, and the weaned child shall put his hand on the adder's den. They shall not hurt nor destroy in all my holy mountain; for the earth shall be full of the knowledge of the LORD, as the waters cover the sea.[9]

In the New Scofield Bible of 1967 the heading above Isaiah 11, which covers verses 1-10, reads, "Davidic kingdom to be restored by Christ: its character and extent." A footnote to verse 1 reads, "This chapter is a prophetic picture of the glory of the future kingdom, which will be set up when David's Son returns in glory." It is obvious, therefore, that the New Scofield Bible interprets this passage as describing the future millennial age.

John F. Walvoord, a representative contemporary premillennialist, shares this interpretation of the chapter:

Isaiah 11 paints the graphic picture of the reign of Christ on earth, a scene which cannot be confused with the present age, the intermediate state, or the eternal state if interpreted in any normal literal sense. As presented it describes the millennial earth. . . . The description [found in this chapter] ... describes animals such as wolves, lambs, leopards, kids, calves, young lions, all of which are creatures of earth and not of heaven, and further pictures them in a time of tranquillity such as only can apply to the millennial earth.[10]

It can easily be understood that if a person believes in a future earthly millennium, he will see that millennium described in these verses. Such an interpretation is, however, by no means the only possible one. We know that the Bible predicts that at the end of time there will be a new earth (see, for example, Is. 65:17; 66:22; Rev. 21:1). Why may we not therefore understand the details found in these verses as descriptions of life on the new earth?[11] This is particularly likely in view of the sweeping panoramic vision conveyed by verse 9: "the earth shall be full of the knowledge of the LORD, as the waters cover the sea." Why should these words have to be thought of as applying only to a thousand-year period preceding the new earth? Do they not picture the final perfection of God's creation?

The other Old Testament passage I should like to adduce in this connection is Isaiah 65:17-25, also quoted from the New Scofield Bible:

(17) For, behold, I create new heavens and a new earth, and the former shall not be remembered, nor come into mind.

(18) But be glad and rejoice forever in that which I create; for, behold, I create Jerusalem a rejoicing, and her people a joy.

(19) And I will rejoice in Jerusalem, and joy in my people; and the voice of weeping shall be no more heard in her, nor the voice of crying.

(20) There shall be no more in it an infant of days, nor an old man that hath not filled his days; for the child shall die an hundred years old, but the sinner, being an hundred

years old, shall be accursed.

(21) And they shall build houses, and inhabit them; and they shall plant vineyards, and eat the fruit of them.

(22) They shall not build, and another inhabit; they shall not plant, and another eat; for like the days of a tree are the days of my people, and mine elect shall long enjoy the work of their hands.

(23) They shall not labor in vain, nor bring forth for trouble; for they are the seed of the blessed of the LORD, and their offspring with them.

(24) And it shall come to pass that, before they call, I will answer; and while they are yet speaking, I will hear.

(25) The wolf and the lamb shall feed together, and the lion shall eat straw like the bullock, and dust shall be the serpent's food. They shall not hurt nor destroy in all my holy mountain, saith the LORD.

In the New Scofield Bible the heading above verse 17 reads, "New heavens and new earth." The heading above verses 18-25, however, reads, "Millennial conditions in the renewed earth with curse removed." It would appear that the editors of this Bible, while compelled to admit that verse 17 describes the final new earth, restrict the meaning of verses 18-25 so as to make them refer only to the millennium which is to precede the final new earth. Walvoord, in similar fashion, understands Isaiah 65:17-19 as describing the eternal state[12] and verses 20-25 of this chapter as describing conditions during the millennium.[13]

Once again it may be observed that if one does not believe in a future earthly millennium, he will certainly not be compelled to accept it by the reading of these verses. If, however, one does believe in such a millennium, he may very well find it described here. But in order to do so he will have to overcome a rather serious exegetical obstacle.

One can find a description of the millennium in this passage only by deliberately overlooking what we find in verses 17-18. Verse 17 speaks unambiguously about the new heavens and the new earth (which the book of Revelation depicts as marking the final state). Verse 18 calls upon the reader to "rejoice forever"—not just for a thousand years—in the new heavens and new earth just referred to. Isaiah is not speaking here about a newness which will last no longer than a thousand years but about an everlasting newness! What follows in verse 19 is linked directly with the preceding: "And I will rejoice in Jerusalem, and joy in my people; and the voice of weeping shall be no more heard in her, nor the voice of crying" (see Rev. 21:4). There is no indication whatever that at this point, or at either verse 18 or 20, Isaiah is suddenly shifting to a description of a millennial age preceding the creation of the new heavens and new earth!

In verse 25, in fact, we have a description of the animal world which reminds us of the picture of the final state found in Isaiah 11. At the end of this verse we hear an echo of what is found in 11:9, "They shall not hurt nor destroy in all my holy mountain, saith the LORD."[14] Truly a beautiful description of the new earth! One will see a millennium here only if he has previously put on his millennial glasses!

A Brief Sketch of Amillennial Eschatology

A common criticism of amillennial eschatology is that it is too negative, spending its strength primarily in opposing and refuting eschatological systems with which it does not agree. Leaving aside the question of whether this criticism is true or false, I would like at this point to counteract the negativism of some amillennial eschatologies by sketching briefly some positive affirmations made by amillennialist theologians. In this way we shall be able to see amillennial eschatology in its totaiity, rather than just as a certain interpretation of the millennium of Revelation 20.

This sketch will cover two areas: first, what amillennial eschatology teaches with regard to *inaugurated eschatology*, and, second, what it teaches with reference to *future eschatology*. By *inaugurated eschatology* I mean that aspect of eschatology which is already present now, during the gospel era. The term *inaugurated eschatology* is preferred to *realized eschatology* because, while the former term does full justice to the fact that the great eschatological incision into history has already been made, it does not rule out a further development and final consummation of eschatology in the future. When we speak of "inaugurated eschatology" we are saying that for the New Testament believer significant eschatological events have already begun to happen while other eschatological occurrences still lie in the future.

As regards *inaugurated eschatology*, then, amillennialism affirms the following:

1. *Christ has won the decisive victory over sin, death and Satan.* By living a sinless life and by dying on the cross as the sacrifice of atonement for our sin, Christ defeated sin. By undergoing death and then victoriously rising from the grave, Christ defeated death. By resisting the devil's temptations, by perfectly obeying God, and by his death and resurrection, Christ delivered a deathblow to Satan and his evil hosts. This victory of Christ's was decisive and final. The most important day in history, therefore, is not the Second Coming of Christ which is still future but the first coming which lies in the past. Because of the victory of Christ, the ultimate issues of history have already been decided. It is now only a question of time until that victory is brought to its final consummation.

2. *The kingdom of God is both present and future.* Amillennialists do not believe that the kingdom of God is primarily a Jewish kingdom which involves the literal restoration of the throne of David. Nor do they believe that because of the unbelief of the Jews of his day Christ postponed the establish-

ment of the kingdom to the time of his future earthly millennial reign. Amillennialists believe that the kingdom of God was founded by Christ at the time of his sojourn on earth, is operative in history now and is destined to be revealed in its fullness in the life to come. They understand the kingdom of God to be the reign of God dynamically active in human history through Jesus Christ. Its purpose is to redeem God's people from sin and from demonic powers, and finally to establish the new heavens and the new earth. The kingdom of God means nothing less than the reign of God in Christ over his entire created universe.

The kingdom of God is therefore both a present reality and a future hope. Jesus clearly taught that the kingdom was already present during his earthly ministry: "But if I drive out demons by the Spirit of God, then the kingdom of God has come upon you" (Mt. 12:28, NIV). When the Pharisees asked Jesus when the kingdom of God was coming, he replied, "The kingdom of God is not coming with signs to be observed; nor will they say, 'Lo, here it is!' or 'There!' for behold, the kingdom of God is in the midst of you" (Lk. 17:20-21). But Jesus also taught that there was a sense in which the kingdom of God was still future, both in specific sayings (Mt. 7:21-23; 8:11-12) and in eschatological parables (such as those of the Marriage Feast, the Tares, the Talents, the Wise and Foolish Virgins). Paul also makes statements describing the kingdom as both present (Rom. 14:17; 1 Cor. 4:19-20; Col. 1:13-14) and future (1 Cor. 6:9; Gal. 5:21; Eph. 5:5; 2 Tim. 4:18).

The fact that the kingdom of God is present in one sense and future in another implies that we who are the subjects of that kingdom live in a kind of tension between the "already" and the "not yet." We are already in the kingdom, and yet we look forward to the full manifestation of that kingdom; we already share its blessings, and yet we await its total victory. Because the exact time when Christ will return is not known, the church must live with a sense of urgency, realizing that the end of history may be very near. At the same time, however, the church must continue to plan and work for a future on this present earth which may still last a long time.

Meanwhile, the kingdom of God demands of us all total commitment to Christ and his cause. We must see all of life and all of reality in the light of the goal of the redemption not just of individuals but of the entire universe. This implies, as Abraham Kuyper, the renowned Dutch theologian and statesman, once said, that there is not a thumb-breadth of the universe about which Christ does not say, "It is mine."

This total commitment further implies a Christian philosophy of history: All of history must be seen as the working out of God's eternal purpose. This kingdom vision includes a Christian philosophy of culture: Art and science, reflecting as they do the glory of God, are to be pursued for his praise. The vision of the kingdom also includes a Christian view of vocation: All callings are from God, and all that we do in everyday life is to be done to God's praise, whether this be study, teaching, preaching, business, industry or housework.

A common source of tension among evangelicals today is the question of whether the church should be primarily concerned with evangelism or social and political action. A proper kingdom vision, it seems to me, will help us to keep our balance on this question. Needless to say, evangelism—bringing people into the kingdom of God—is one of the essential tasks of the church. But since the kingdom of God demands total commitment, the church must also be vitally concerned about the implementation of Christian principles in every area of life, including the political and the social. Evangelism and social concern, therefore, must never be thought of as options between which Christians may make a choice; both are essential to full-orbed kingdom obedience.

3. *Though the last day is still future, we are in the last days now.*

This aspect of eschatology, which is often neglected in evangelical circles, is an essential part of the New Testament message. When I say, "we are in the last days now," I understand the expression "the last days" not merely as referring to the time just before Christ's return, but as a description of the entire era between Christ's first and second comings. New Testament writers were conscious of the fact that they were already living in the last days at the time they were speaking or writing. This was specifically stated by Peter in his sermon on the day of Pentecost when he quoted Joel's prophecy about the pouring out of the Spirit upon all flesh in the last days (Acts 2:16-17). He was thus saying in effect, "We are now in the last days predicted by the prophet Joel." Paul made the same point when he described believers of his day as those "upon whom the end of the ages has come" (1 Cor. 10:11). And the Apostle John told his readers that they were already living in "the last hour" (1 Jn. 2:18). In the light of these New Testament teachings, we may indeed speak of an inaugurated eschatology, while remembering that the Bible also speaks of a final consummation of eschatological events in what John commonly calls "the last day" (Jn. 6:39-40, 44, 54; 11:24; 12:48).

The fact that we are living in the last days now implies that we are already tasting the beginnings of eschatological blessings—that, as Paul says, we already have "the first fruits of the Spirit" (Rom. 8:23). This means that we who are believers are to see ourselves not as impotent sinners who are helpless in the face of temptation but as new creatures in Christ (2 Cor. 5:17), as temples of the Holy Spirit (1 Cor. 6:19) and as those who have decisively crucified the flesh (Gal. 5:24), put off the old self and put on the new (Col. 3:9-10). All this involves having an image of ourselves which is primarily positive rather than negative. It also involves seeing fellow Christians as those who are in Christ with us and for whom we should therefore thank God.[15]

4. *As far as the thousand years of Revelation 20 are concerned, we are in the millennium now.* Earlier in the chapter evidence was given for the position that the thousand years of Revelation 20 extend from the first coming of Christ to just before his Second Coming, when Satan will be loosed for a short time. The amillennial position on the thousand years of Revelation 20 implies that Christians who are now living are enjoying the benefits of this millennium since Satan has been bound for the duration of this period. As we saw, the fact that Satan is now bound does not mean that he is not active in the world today but that during this period he cannot deceive the nations—that is, cannot prevent the spread of the gospel. The binding of Satan during this era, in other words, makes missions and evangelism possible. This fact should certainly be a source of encouragement to the church on earth.

Amillennials also teach that during this same thousand-year period the souls of believers who have died are now living and reigning with Christ in heaven while they await the resurrection of the body. Their state is therefore a state of blessedness and happiness, though their joy will not be complete until their bodies have been raised. This teaching should certainly bring comfort to those whose dear ones have died in the Lord.

As regards *future eschatology,* amillennialism affirms the following:

1. *The "signs of the times" have both present and future relevance.* Amillennialists believe that the return of Christ will be preceded by certain signs: for example, the preaching of the gospel to all the nations, the conversion of the fullness of Israel, the great apostasy, the great tribulation and the coming of the Antichrist. These signs, however, must not be thought of as referring exclusively to the time just preceding Christ's return. They have been present in some sense from the very beginning of the Christian era[16] and are present now.[17] This

means that we must always be ready for the Lord's return and that we may never in our thoughts push the return of Christ off into the far-distant future.

Amillennialists also believe, however, that these "signs of the times" will have a climactic final fulfillment just before Christ returns. This fulfillment will not take the form of phenomena which are totally new but will rather be an intensification of signs which have been present all along.

2. *The Second Coming of Christ will be a single event.* Amillennialists find no scriptural basis for the dispensationalist division of the Second Coming into two phases (sometimes called the *parousia* and the *revelation*), with a seven-year period in between. We understand Christ's return as being a single event.

3. *At the time of Christ's return, there will be a general resurrection, both of believers and unbelievers.* Amillennialists reject the common premillennial teaching that the resurrection of believers and that of unbelievers will be separated by a thousand years. They also reject the view of many dispensationalists that there will be as many as three or four resurrections (since, in addition to the two resurrections just mentioned, dispensationalists also teach that there will be a resurrection of tribulation saints and a resurrection of believers who died during the millennium). We see no scriptural evidence for such multiple resurrections.[18]

4. *After the resurrection, believers who are then still alive shall suddenly be transformed and glorified.* The basis for this teaching is what Paul says in 1 Corinthians 15:51-52: "Listen, I tell you a mystery: We shall not all sleep, but we shall all be changed—in a flash, in the twinkling of an eye, at the last trumpet. For the trumpet will sound, the dead will be raised imperishable, and we shall be changed" (NIV).

5. *The "rapture" of all believers now takes place.* Believers who have just been raised from the dead, together with living be-

lievers who have just been transformed, are now caught up in the clouds to meet the Lord in the air (1 Thess. 4:17). That there will be such a "rapture" the Bible clearly teaches. But I have put the word *rapture* between quotation marks in order to distinguish the amillennial conception of the rapture from the dispensationalist view. Dispensationalists teach that after the rapture the entire church will be taken up to heaven for a period of seven years while those still on earth are undergoing the great tribulation.

Amillennialists see no scriptural evidence for such a seven-year period or for a transference of the church from earth to heaven during that period. Risen and glorified bodies of believers do not belong in heaven but on the earth. The word translated "to meet" in 1 Thessalonians 4:17 (*apantēsis*) is a technical term used in the days of the New Testament to describe a public welcome given by a city to a visiting dignitary. People would ordinarily leave the city to meet the distinguished visitor and then go back with him into the city.[19] On the basis of the analogy conveyed by this word, all Paul is saying here is that raised and transformed believers are caught up in the clouds to meet the descending Lord, implying that after this meeting they will go back with him to the earth.

6. *Now follows the final judgment.* Whereas dispensationalists commonly teach that there will be at least three separate judgments, amillennialists do not agree. The latter see scriptural evidence for only one Day of Judgment which will occur at the time of Christ's return. All men must then appear before the judgment seat of Christ.

The purpose of the final judgment is not primarily to determine the final destiny of men since by that time that final destiny has already been determined for all men except those still living at the time of Christ's return. Rather, the judgment will have a threefold purpose: First, it will reveal the glorification of God in the final destiny assigned to each person; sec-

ond, it will indicate finally and publicly the great antithesis of
history between the people of God and the enemies of God;
and third, it will reveal the degree of reward or the degree
of punishment which each shall receive.

7. *After the judgment the final state is ushered in.* Unbelievers
and all those who have rejected Christ shall spend eternity in
hell, whereas believers will enter into everlasting glory on the
new earth. The concept of the new earth is so important for
biblical eschatology that we should give it more than a passing
thought. Many Christians think of themselves as spending
eternity in some ethereal heaven while the Bible plainly
teaches us that there will be a new earth. When the book of
Revelation tells us that the holy city, the new Jerusalem, will
come down from heaven to the new earth (21:2), that God will
now have his dwelling with men (21:3) and that the throne of
God and of the Lamb will be in the new Jerusalem (22:3), it is
teaching us in figurative language that in the life to come
heaven and earth will no longer be separated but will have
merged. In the final state, therefore, glorified believers will be
both in heaven and on the new earth, since the two shall then
be one.

When one keeps the vision of the new earth clearly in mind,
many biblical teachings begin to form a significant pattern.
As we have seen, the resurrection of the body calls for a new
earth. The cosmic significance of the work of Christ implies
that the curse which came upon creation because of man's sin
(Gen. 3:17-19) shall some day be removed (Rom. 8:19-22);
this renewal of creation means that there will indeed be a new
earth. The Bible also contains specific promises about the new
earth. We have already looked at Isaiah's prediction of the
new earth in 65:17 (see 66:22). Jesus promised that the meek
shall inherit the earth (Mt. 5:5). Peter speaks of new heavens
and a new earth in which righteousness shall dwell (2 Pet. 3:
13). And the elders and living creatures whom John sees in the

heavenly vision recorded in Revelation 5 sing a song of praise to the victorious Lamb which includes these words, "You have made them [those whom you purchased with your blood] to be a kingdom and priests to serve our God, and they will reign on the earth" (**Rev. 5:10, NIV**).[20]

In the light of biblical teaching about the new earth, many Old Testament prophecies about the land of Canaan and about the future of the people of God fall into place. From the fourth chapter of the book of Hebrews we learn that Canaan was a type of the Sabbath-rest of the people of God in the life to come. From Paul's letter to the Galatians we learn that all those who are in Christ are included in the seed of Abraham (Gal. 3:29). When we read Genesis 17:8 ("And I will give unto thee, and to thy seed after thee, the land of thy sojournings, all the land of Canaan, for an everlasting possession; and I will be their God" [ASV]) with this understanding of the New Testament broadening of these concepts, we see in it a promise of the new earth as the everlasting possession of all the people of God, not just of the physical descendants of Abraham. And when, in the light of this New Testament teaching, we now read Amos 9:15 ("And I will plant them upon their land, and they shall no more be plucked up out of their land which I have given them, saith Jehovah thy God" [ASV]), we do not feel compelled to restrict the meaning of these words to national Israel and the land of Palestine. We understand them to be a prediction of the eternal dwelling of all God's people, Gentiles as well as Jews, on the new earth of which Canaan was a type. Amillennialists therefore feel no need for positing an earthly millennium to provide for the fulfillment of prophecies of this sort; they see such prophecies as pointing to the glorious eternal future which awaits all the people of God.

When premillennialists therefore charge amillennialists with teaching a future kingdom which is only spiritual and

which has nothing to do with the earth, they are not representing the amillennial view correctly. Amillennialists believe that
Old Testament prophecies which predict that the land of promise shall be the everlasting possession of the people of God,
that the wolf shall dwell with the lamb and that the earth shall
be as full of the knowledge of the Lord as the waters cover
the sea, shall be fulfilled not just for a thousand-year period
but for all eternity! This interpretation, we believe, gives us a
richer, wider and more relevant understanding of those
prophecies than that which restricts their meaning to a description of an earthly millennium which shall precede the
final state.

Some Implications of Amillennial Eschatology

What, in conclusion, are some of the implications of amillennial eschatology for our theological understanding? Let me
mention four of them:

1. *What binds the Old and New Testaments together is the unity
of the covenant of grace.* Amillennialists do not believe that sacred history is to be divided into a series of distinct and dis-
parate dispensations but see a single covenant of grace run-
ning through all of that history. This covenant of grace is still
in effect today and will culminate in the eternal dwelling together of God and his redeemed people on the new earth.

2. *The kingdom of God is central in human history.* That kingdom was predicted and prepared for in Old Testament times,
was established on earth by Jesus Christ, was extended and expanded both in New Testament times and during the subse-
quent history of the church, and will finally be consummated
in the life to come.

3. *Jesus Christ is the Lord of history.* This means that all of history is under Christ's control and will ultimately prove to have
been subservient to his purpose. We must therefore be concerned not just with enjoying the blessings of our salvation but

also with joyfully serving Christ as Lord in every area of our lives.

4. *All of history is moving toward a goal: the total redemption of the universe.* History is not meaningless but meaningful. Though we are not always able to discern the meaning of each historical event, we know what the ultimate outcome of history will be. We eagerly look forward to the new earth as part of a renewed universe in which God's good creation will realize finally and totally the purpose for which he called it into existence: the glorification of his name.

All this implies that regarding world history, amillennialists adopt a position of *sober or realistic optimism*. Belief in the present rule of Christ, in the presence of God's kingdom and in the movement of history toward its goal is accompanied by a realistic recognition of the presence of sin in this world and of the growing development of the kingdom of evil. Amillennial eschatology looks for a culmination of apostasy and tribulation in the final emergence of a personal Antichrist before Christ comes again. Amillennialists do not expect to see the perfect society realized during this present age.

Yet, since we know that the victory of Christ over evil was decisive and that Christ is now on the throne, the dominant mood of amillennial eschatology is optimism—Christian optimism. This means that we view no world crisis as totally beyond help and no social trend as absolutely irreversible. It means that we live in hope—a hope that is built on faith and that expresses itself in love.

Amillennial eschatology, therefore, gives us a realistic, yet basically optimistic world-and-life view. It is an eschatology which is exciting, exhilarating and challenging. It is an eschatology which gives us an inspiring vision of the lordship of Christ over history and of the ultimate triumph of his kingdom.

AN HISTORIC PREMILLENNIAL RESPONSE
GEORGE ELDON LADD

I am in agreement with practically all that Hoekema has written with the exception of his exegesis of Revelation 20. I agree that Matthew 12:29 clearly teaches that the earthly ministry of Jesus meant the invasion of the kingdom of God into history which in turn meant a binding of Satan. However, this is different from the binding of Satan in Revelation 20. The former meant the breaking of the power of Satan that individual men and women might be delivered from his control. The latter binding meant that he should deceive the nations no more.

That John saw the "souls of those who had been beheaded" does not prove that the scene is in heaven. In fact it is very difficult to know throughout the Revelation when John is in heaven and when he is on earth. In this context, however, John distinctly says that he "saw an angel coming down from heaven" (Rev. 20:1) thereby affirming that the scene has shifted from heaven to earth. And if the statement "they came to life" (Rev. 20:4) means, as we believe, bodily resurrection, then the scene is the earth.

I admit that the greatest difficulty to any premillennialism ıs the fact that most of the New Testament pictures the consummation as occurring at Jesus' parousia. However, if one believes in progressive revelation, this is no insuperable problem. The Old Testament does not foresee or precisely predict the Church Age. It sees the future exclusively in terms of Israel as the people of God. Therefore, the fact that the New Testament in only *one* place teaches an interim kingdom, between this age and the Age to Come is no reason for rejecting ıt.

I feel that Hoekema does not meet the demands of exegesis for three reasons. The first has already been spelled out in my own essay. Revelation 19—20 appears to be continuous and describes the destruction of the evil triumvirate: first the beast, then the false prophet (19:20-21) and then the power behind these two—the devil. There is absolutely no hint of any recapitulation in chapter 20.

A second reason is that the verb translated "they came to life" (*ezēsan*, Rev. 20:4-5) is never in the New Testament used of life after death, *except in resurrection*. The word can be used of coming to life spiritually (Jn. 5:25)—indeed, Paul describes life in terms of resurrection and ascension with Christ (Eph. 2:6). But it is never used elsewhere of the soul living on after the death of the body. On the contrary, various forms of the verb are used of resurrection life on numerous occasions referring to men in general (Mt. 9:18; Acts 9:41; 20:12), as well as of Jesus (Lk. 24:5, 23; Acts 1:3; Rom. 14:9; 2 Cor. 13:4). The same verb is used in Revelation 2:8 of Jesus' resurrection: "who died and came to life."

Third, Hoekema has a rather unusual interpretation of Revelation 20:5. This verse has usually been understood to refer to bodily resurrection, and Hoekema's exegesis of this verse avoids the criticism leveled against it in my essay. Hoekema argues that *neither* 20:5 nor 20:6 refers to bodily resurrection. In this he is consistent. However, I cannot follow his exegesis of 20:5. He reads it to mean, "The unbelieving dead ... did not live or reign with Christ during this thousand-year period" (p. 170). This however is not what the text says. "The rest of the dead did not come to life [did not live] until the thousand years were ended." A natural reading of the text clearly suggests that after the thousand years the rest of the dead did come to life. "Until" (*achri*) clearly implies this. Hoekema's effort to get around the natural meaning of the text is completely unconvincing.

I remain, therefore, a convinced premillennialist.

A DISPENSATIONAL PREMILLENNIAL RESPONSE
HERMAN A. HOYT

The writer presenting the amillennial view has wisely arranged the order of his discussion to prepare the reader for the salient features of his discussion. The particular interpretation he gives to the book of Revelation is absolutely essential as a background for the discussion he gives to Revelation 20: 1-6 in which he removes the millennium as a future possibility after the return of Christ. This is logically followed by a discussion of two passages of Scripture in which he seeks to refute the principle of literal interpretation as the only valid hermeneutic for understanding the Scriptures. This prepares the way for sketching the movement of amillennial eschatology with its implications.

I appreciate some of the clear distinctions Hoekema makes concerning the amillennial position. In one sense he is right in deprecating the connotation in the term *amillennial*. Other terms have been proposed but fall short in striking at the central issue involved. So the term *amillennial* is retained and defined. Even though it seems inappropriate from one standpoint, yet from another it more clearly indicates that those who hold this view do not believe that there is an earthly millennium ushered in at the Second Coming of Christ which will run its course before the introduction of the eternal state.

The interpretation of the book of Revelation lays the foundation for the doctrine of amillennialism. Hoekema frankly says,

> Let us assume, for example, that the book of Revelation is to be interpreted in an exclusively futuristic sense, referring only to events that are to happen around or at the time of Christ's Second Coming. Let us further assume that what is presented in Revelation 20 must necessarily follow, in chronological order, what was described in chapter 19. We are then virtually compelled to believe that the thousand-year reign depicted in 20:4 must come after the return of Christ described in 19:11. (p. 156)

This appears to be a fatal admission and raises the serious question as to the validity of the method in interpreting the book of Revelation.

Hoekema adopts the view of *progressive parallelism* used by William Hendriksen in his commentary on Revelation. This consists of seven sections which run parallel to each other, each supposedly depicting the church and the world from the time of Christ's first coming to the time of his Second Coming. This divides the book of Revelation as follows: chapters 1—3; 4—7; 8—11; 12—14; 15—16; 17—19; and 20—22. This strategy makes the incarceration of Satan fall at the first coming of Christ (20:1-3), and 20:4-6 describes the millennial reign as coming before the return of Christ to execute resurrection and judgment (20:11-15). This eliminates the millennium as a period of time occurring after the return of Christ. The only sense in which the millennium dare be construed in this interpretation is that expanse of time intervening between the first and second comings of Christ.

As Hoekema sincerely admits, this method of handling the book of Revelation "is not without its difficulties," even though it seems most satisfactory to him. But this is a way of getting rid of futuristic implications in the book of Revelation and also of escaping any literalism that might be embarrassing to his system. This is this method of giving historical interpretation to the book of Revelation. But however scholastic the reasoning, difficulties do not go away that easily. Even though the book of Revelation is apocalyptic this does not mean that it becomes obscure. This method of presentation only makes it more vivid. The imagery, however, must be interpreted in terms of the Bible, and this imagery must be understandable to the average person. Moreover, far less in this book is figurative than many are wanting it to be. To the average person the effort to move the millennium to a place before the Second Coming of Christ is demanding the human mind to accede to something that does not appear on the face of the text. But even more than that, the effort to make seven divisions cover the same period of time (between the first and second comings) will meet with all sorts of confusion to establish its validity. At best this is a shaky foundation upon which to establish a firm doctrine of amillennialism.

In discussing Revelation 20:1-6 Hoekema makes a number of assertions that are difficult to support from the passage. The interpreter may not only "safely" conclude that the thousand years of verses 1-3 and 4-6 are the same, but he is compelled to draw that conclusion. The Greek language uses the definite article in four instances (vv. 3, 5-7). This is to call attention to the fact that this is the same period under discussion. He asserts that verses 1-3 have to do with the earth and that verses 4-6 have to do with heaven. But there is nothing in the text which demands that conclusion. If verses 1-3 have to do with the earth, so also do verses 4-6. And a parallel passage seems to argue for reigning on the earth (Rev. 5:10). The scene in Revelation 6:9-11 can hardly be adduced to support the point he is making, for that scene is clearly set in heaven (Rev. 4—6).

In order to escape a contradiction of the Scriptures in support of amillennialism, Hoekema must remove any possibility for two physical resurrections to be understood in verses 4-6 of chapter 20. He must concede that John is speaking of "a kind of resurrection here" (p. 168) because the Scriptures use the word *resurrection*. But he must insist that this is not a resurrection before the millennium and another after the millennium, even though the text seems to say that. His reason is that there is just one resurrection, and it comes after the ushering in of the eternal state at the Second Coming, and it includes both believers and unbelievers. To establish his conclusion that this is a general judgment he cites John 5: 28-29 and Acts 24:15. But these passages do not prove a general judgment. All they do is assert that both wicked and righteous will be raised. The time is not stated. In Revelation 20:5 the time element is stated. Revelation 20:11-15 has to do with the wicked. This means that verses 4-6 deal specifically with the righteous (and the words "came to life" must be taken in the normal sense of physical resurrection) and that they will reign bodily on the earth, not as spirits ruling and reigning from heaven in this present time before the Second Coming of Christ, as Hoekema declares.

In discussing the condition of Satan as set forth in 20:1-3, Hoekema explains that Satan was bound at the first coming of Christ, was defeated by the work of Christ on the cross and is now experiencing certain relative limitations to his activity. He is not now deceiving the nations, as he did before Christ came, so that believers are free to disseminate the gospel among the nations. This binding does not mean that Satan cannot do any harm. His restriction applies only to deceiving the nations, a restriction which will be removed at the Second Coming of Christ at which time he will meet his final doom. During this gospel age he is bound and cannot prevent the spread of the gospel nor gather all the enemies of Christ together to attack the church. Though several passages are cited to prove that Satan is bound during this gospel period (Mt. 12:28-29; Lk. 10:17-18; Jn. 12:31-32), they are hardly convincing on the point at issue.

Seeking refuge in the right to spiritualize Scripture, two passages from the Old Testament bearing on the millennium are cited (Is. 11:6-9; 65:17-25). Except for Is. 65:17 the notes in the Scofield Reference Bible assign them to the millennium. Hoekema believes that all these verses describe the eternal state because in his estimation the only millennium the Bible talks about is the period between the first and second comings of Christ, and these passages do not describe conditions in this present time. But if it is understood that the mediatorial or millennial kingdom will merge into the eternal state, then this description could be true of both. Isaiah 65:17 does make reference to a new heaven and a new earth. The change initiated in the millennium will be so amazing that it is like a new heaven and a new earth, and this change will reach its fullest stage in the eternal state. There is no reason then why some of the changes noted in the passage are not true of the millennium and others of the eternal state, and thus no contradiction in the ensuing verses (Is. 65:18-25).

Generally I found myself in agreement with Hoekema's sketch of amillennial eschatology. Christ did win a decisive victory over sin, death and Satan at his first coming. Not all the benefits have been ushered into experience. The full effects are yet future. The kingdom of God in the universal sense is operative, and most certainly a spiritual aristocracy is being conscripted for the future. We are now living in the last days and have been since the first coming of Christ (Acts 2:16-17; 1 Cor. 10:11; 1 Jn. 2:18). I am in perfect agreement that these days constitute an inaugurated eschatology while at the same time remembering a final consummation lies ahead called "the last day" (Jn. 6:39-40, 44, 54; 11:24; 12:48). This means that believers are tasting the blessings of the future such as "the first fruits of the Spirit" (Rom. 8:23). And it further means that there is urgency of responsibility resting upon believers (2 Cor. 5:17; 1 Cor. 6:19; Gal. 5:24; Col. 3:9-10). But I cannot agree that we are now living in the millennium as set forth in Scripture.

Hoekema is certainly right that there are "signs of the times" pointing to the future, a future that may be very near at hand. Though he believes that the Second Coming of Christ is a single event, I hold that it is a complex event covering an extended period of time and consisting of two phases. The Scriptures do not support the doctrine of a general resurrection and a general judgment. At least a thousand years intervene between the resurrection of the righteous and the wicked. Hoekema finds no place for a seven-year interval between the resurrection of the church and Christ's return to establish his kingdom. Thus there is no rapture of the church in the sense of absence during that awful period described as tribulation. In his opinion the Scriptures teach that Christ will come a second time to consummate the tribulation, rapture the church, raise all the dead, perform judgment upon all and usher in the eternal state. He does believe that the New Jerusalem will come to earth and the new earth will be the home of the redeemed throughout eternity with God dwelling with mankind in the person of his Son.

It is reassuring to contemplate the implications of amillennialism as listed by Hoekema. One pervading covenant of grace binds the Old and New Testaments into a unity. With this I agree. But I believe that this one covenant has its varied phases, with which Hoekema does not agree. The kingdom of God is central in human history, and it will at last be consummated in the eternal state. Most certainly Christ is the Lord of history. History is his story and he is guiding it toward that final goal, a goal which he is accomplishing through redemption for the entire universe. All this provides a spirit of optimism for the believer in the midst of the darkest hours of history.

A POSTMILLENNIAL RESPONSE
LORAINE BOETTNER

There is comparatively little difference between postmillennialism and amillennialism, at least when either of these is compared with historic premillennialism or dispensationalism. Briefly, postmillennialism holds that the kingdom of God is now being extended in the world through the preaching of the gospel and the saving work of the Holy Spirit, that the world eventually will be Christianized and that the return of Christ will occur at the close of a long period of righteousness and peace. Amillennialism holds that the Bible does not predict any such period of righteousness and peace before the return of Christ but that there will be a parallel and contemporaneous development of good and evil, God's kingdom and Satan's kingdom, which will continue until the Second Coming of Christ. Both postmillennialism and amillennialism hold that the Second Coming of Christ will be followed immediately by the resurrection and judgment, and the eternal order of things.

Many people simply cannot believe that the world is getting better. But we should remember that as far as evil is concerned, that has been the natural condition of the world ever since the fall of the race in Adam. At the time Christ came, nearly two thousand years ago, the entire world, with the exception of the little land of Palestine, was in heathen darkness. But since that time the gospel has been progressively carried throughout the world, and today there are tens of millions of true Christians. The marvel is not that there is so much evil in the world but that there is so much righteousness. Christian principles are widely recognized as those by which people and nations *should* live and be governed, even though they are as yet very inconsistently applied.

While we do not yet see a Christianized world, we do see the church making great progress and uplifting mankind as it becomes effective in ever-widening areas. And if Christianity has already brought about the marvelous changes that we see in so many areas, what must it be when that benign influence is extended throughout the entire world!

Hoekema's exposition of amillennialism is centered primarily on the twentieth chapter of the book of Revelation since the millennium is mentioned nowhere else in the Bible. His method of interpreting this book seems very commendable to me, as does also his method of interpreting Old Testament prophecy. He divides the book of Revelation into seven sections which run parallel to each other, each of which narrates in a different way the progress of the church between the first and second comings of Christ.

I believe, however, that Revelation 19:11-21 describes not the Second Coming of Christ, as he briefly indicates, but rather that it describes the progress of the church between the first and second comings of Christ. This section uses the imagery of a great battle in which two mighty contending forces are engaged. This, I believe, is a battle that rages through the centuries, even through the millenniums, as Christ on his heavenly throne directs the affairs of his kingdom on earth—the outward manifestation of which is the church. And it results in an overwhelming victory for him and his church.

Whereas amillennialism does not look for a Christianized world before the return of Christ, let us consider two quite prosaic statements in the Gospel of Matthew which have a bearing on this subject. The first of these is the Great Commission given by Christ to his disciples in Matthew 28:18-20.

And Jesus came and said to them, "All authority in heaven and on earth has been given to me. Go therefore and make disciples of all nations, baptizing them in the name of the Father and of the Son and of the Holy Spirit, teaching them to observe all that I have commanded you; and lo, I am with you always, to the close of the age."

In those words we are told that *all authority in heaven and on earth* has been given to the ascended and reigning Christ. And on the basis of that authority he has commanded his followers to go and *make disciples of all nations.* To that end he has promised that he will be with them always, even to the end of the world. His purpose therefore during the Church Age is the Christianizing of the world. He can never have any more power than he has now for the carrying out of that project even if he were to come, as the premillennialists believe, and set up a thousand-year kingdom in the city of Jerusalem. His disciples are to go and teach the people all things that he has commanded them. Therefore this cannot be a merely external or superficial announcement or "witness" concerning the gospel but an effectively taught system of truth that changes lives. Those who become disciples are to be baptized. But only true believers are ever to be baptized.

Do we have any right to expect him to return for his church before it has accomplished its assigned work? I do not believe so. Surely the bridegroom will not come for his bride before she has made herself ready! Therefore we believe that the work assigned to the church in the Great Commission means that the world will eventually be Christianized, even as that is set forth on postmillennial principles.

The second reference which teaches that the world is to be Christianized is Matthew 16:18. It reads, "And I say unto thee, That thou art Peter, and upon this rock I will build my church: and the gates of hell shall not prevail against it" (AV). This verse immediately follows Peter's magnificent confession of Jesus as the Christ. The statement that the gates of hell will not be able to prevail against the church has usually been understood to mean that the church will be able to defend itself against all its foes, that even the worst that the enemies of the gospel can bring against it will not be able to destroy it. We believe, however, that the real meaning is quite different.

Gates are not offensive, but defensive weapons. They are stationary. They are not used to make an attack. In that day the gates of a city were strongly fortified instruments designed to withstand even the strongest onslaughts of the attackers. As such they did not move. Hence the real meaning of this verse is that the church will take the offensive, that it will advance throughout the world and that nothing, literally nothing, will be able to resist its onward march. Not even the fortress of hell itself will be able to resist. Before the end comes the church will make a clean sweep of everything. This of course does not mean that all evil will be eliminated, for all who enter this world are born unregenerate sons of Adam and are totally dependent on the grace of God for cleansing. But how harmoniously this general picture fits in with the overwhelming victory ascribed to the rider of the white horse in Revelation 19:11-21! Surely this speaks volumes for the postmillennial rather than the amillennial or the premillennial position.

Hoekema's interpretation of the very important section, Revelation 20:1-6, is, I believe, essentially correct. He says that verses 1-3 take us back to the beginning of the New Testament era, the defeat of Satan having been accomplished at the first coming of Christ, at which time Satan was bound for a thousand years. He was bound not in the sense that he can no longer do any evil but only that he can no longer keep the gospel from being preached to the nations of the world as had been the case in pre-Christian times. The thousand years means not an exact period of that length but an indefinitely long time—actually the period between the first and the second comings of Christ. Now that spell has been broken, and the gospel is being preached to all the nations.

Verses 4-6 also speak of a thousand-year period which evidently continues throughout the entire Church Age. And since the souls there spoken of are the souls of believers who have been "beheaded," it is quite clear that, as Hoekema says, the locale in John's vision is now shifted from earth to heaven. Since persecution and martyrdom were so common in John's day, that figure of having been beheaded probably is intended to include all believers who remain true to their Lord till death. And since John saw them sitting on thrones, that evidently means that they were reigning with Christ and would continue to reign with him from the time of their death on through the rest of the interadventual period.

But Hoekema says that certain signs (such as the preaching of the gospel to all the nations, the conversion of the Jews, the great apostasy, the great tribulation and the coming of Antichrist) must precede the return of Christ. He then adds that those signs have relevance not only to the future but also to the present since they have been with us in some sense from the beginning of the Christian era. This seems to me to leave such signs practically meaningless. How are we to know when such signs have reached a sufficient degree of intensity to indicate that the Lord's return is at hand?

Regarding the preaching of the gospel to the nations as a sign of the end, great advances have been made at various times (such as during the Apostolic Age, the time of Augustine, the Protestant Reformation, and the revivals under Whitefield and the Wesleys), each making great advances over anything that had gone before, but each being followed by periods of inertia or apostasy. During our twentieth century there has been a tremendous advance in the spread of the gospel. Through the work of great church organizations as well as many independent agencies, and through the use of the printing press, radio, and television, the gospel today is literally being carried to all the nations of the world. But who can say that this present, large-scale work is a sign of the end?

As for the conversion of the Jews as a sign of the near return of the Lord, only a comparatively small proportion of world Jewry has turned to Christianity, which might indicate that the end is still far away. And yet the conversion of a considerable number of the Jews, and especially the return of a substantial number of them to Palestine and the formation of the state of Israel, has led many to believe that the Lord's return is very near.

The so-called great apostasy is another matter concerning which there is much difference of opinion. There have been numerous times when it seemed that the light of the gospel would go out. We need mention only the barbaric invasions and the fall of Rome in the fifth century, the Dark Ages which preceded the Protestant Reformation, and the Inquisition in Spain and Italy and elsewhere when tens of thousands were put to death by torturous means for their faith. But none of those, severe as they were, was a true sign of the Lord's return. After each the church recovered and made much greater advances.

Much tribulation has also been present at various times, with great severity and over large areas. We think especially of the Mohammedan invasion in the seventh and eighth centuries which swept across all of the Near East, up into Europe as far as Italy and Austria, across all of North Africa, across

Spain and into France. The Black Plague ravaged Asia and Europe in the fourteenth century. The Thirty Years War devastated much of central Europe in the seventeenth century. There have been two so-called World Wars in our twentieth century. For a time each of those seemed to qualify as great tribulation. But after each there was recovery and greater advances.

As for the Antichrist, various ones have been temporarily cast in that role: Attila the Hun in the fifth century; the pope at the time of the Protestant Reformation; Napoleon in the nineteenth century; Mussolini, Hitler and Stalin in the twentieth century.

And so it goes. All such signs are admittedly relative and more or less prominent in every age. I do not believe that any such signs can properly be regarded as proofs or even indications that the return of Christ is near. Rather, I believe that the signs mentioned in Matthew 24:1-34 related to the then coming destruction of Jerusalem, which occurred in A.D. 70. These have therefore long since had their fulfillment. For verse 34 reads, "Truly, I say to you, this generation will not pass away till all these things take place." J. Marcellus Kik, in *An Eschatology of Victory*, has given a detailed exposition of this chapter. I would strongly recommend that book for all who are interested in that subject.

Hoekema, in true amillennial fashion, is noncommital regarding the time of Christ's return. He says, "Because the exact time when Christ will return is not known, the church must live with a sense of urgency, realizing that the end of history may be very near." But then he adds, "At the same time, however, the church must continue to plan and work for a future on this present earth which may still last a long time" (p. 179).

An objection commonly put to postmillennialism, teaching that the return of Christ probably is yet in the far distant future, is that if that is true, we cannot properly "watch" for his coming as we are so clearly commanded to do. But that objection is answered by the fact that there are various ways in which Christ comes. I think that it is unfortunate that of the many books that deal with the coming of Christ, most of them ignore or even scoff at the idea that there are other ways in which he comes besides his final, visible coming. Consider the following:

1. *The coming of Christ for the Christian at the time of death.* Jesus said, "I go to prepare a place for you. And if I go and prepare a place for you, I will come again, and receive you unto myself" (Jn. 14:2-3, AV). There is a coming of Christ for the faithful believer at the time of death, as he welcomes into the heavenly kingdom one whom he has purchased at so great a price, one for whom he died personally and with whom he will spend eternity. And that entrance into the heavenly kingdom certainly will be the most climactic event in the believer's entire existence. This is a coming which provides an opportunity to watch as fully the equivalent of the Second Coming because we know that for each of us that event will be in the comparatively near future and that we should be ready for it at all times. Surely that is the coming with which we as individuals should be most concerned.

2. *The coming of Christ in judgment.* In Matthew 24 we have a prediction of Christ's coming in judgment on the apostate nation of Israel, which occurred in the year A.D. 70. Verse 34, quoted above, fixes very definitely the time of that coming.

3. *The coming of Christ to the disciples after his resurrection.* This was a literal, visible, personal coming. In his last discourse he said, "I will not leave you desolate; I come unto you"; and "Ye heard how I said to you, I go away, and I will come to you" (Jn. 14:18; see also 14:28); and again, "A little while, and you will see me no more; again a little while, and you will see me" (Jn. 16:16). As the events proved, his several appearances after his resurrection were literal comings to them personally.

4. *The coming of Christ on the day of Pentecost.* In the events of that day Christ providentially manifested his presence in human affairs with a great outpouring of his Spirit through which he displayed his power and enlightened and equipped the apostles to be world evangelists.

5. *The coming of Christ to the churches in Asia Minor.* To the church in Ephesus he gave this warning: "Remember then from what you have fallen, repent and do the works you did at first. If not I will come to you and remove your lampstand from its place, unless you repent" (Rev. 2:5). Similar warnings were given to other churches in Asia Minor. The church in Ephesus did not repent; he did come; and he did remove its lampstand and that church ceased to exist. That of course was not a visible coming, but it was nevertheless a predicted and a very real coming.

6. *The coming of Christ to believers, and a presence of Christ through the Spirit with believers in all ages.* Christ said, "If a man loves me, he will keep my word, and my Father will love him and we will come unto him and make our home with him ' (Jn. 14:23). And again, "Where two or three are gathered in m name, there am I in the midst of them" (Mt. 18:20).

7. *The coming of Christ to various cities in Palestine during his public ministry.* When the twelve were sent out on a preaching mission, he told them, "You will not have gone through all the towns of Israel, before the Son of man comes" (Mt. 10:23). He evidently meant that he would visit those same cities shortly for we are told that soon afterward he "appointed seventy others, and sent them on ahead of him, two by two, into every town and place where he himself was about to come" (Lk. 10:1).

8. *And finally, the visible, glorious coming of Christ at the end of the age.* This most important and climactic coming was promised by two angels at the time of Christ's ascension and is acknowledged by all Christians.

Keeping in mind the distinctive tenets of postmillennialism (that over the centuries the church of Christ is winning the victory over all other systems and that eventually Christ will return to a Christianized world), I should like to close with a quotation from Kenneth Scott Latourette, perhaps the greatest of church historians. In his monumental work, *A History of the Extension of Christianity*, in the concluding chapter of volume seven, he says,

In the past hundred and fifty years Christianity has had its greatest geographic extension and its widest influence upon mankind. Through its history it has gone forward by major pulsations. Each advance has carried it further than the one before. Of the alternating recessions, each has been briefer and less marked than the one which preceded it.

He then asks, "Is there warrant in history for confidence in the dogma of progress, so fondly cherished by man in the nineteenth century?" He answers,

It may well be that in the course of the centuries Christianity will become the professed faith of all mankind. If this comes, presumably it will be only after a vast reach of time. ... It is of the very core of the Christian faith that the God and Father of his Lord, Jesus Christ, will not be defeated.

He adds, however, that this does not mean that all men the world over will ever be brought to full conformity to the Christian pattern for the simple reason that perfection is not attainable in this life. Yet who among those holding to other systems of eschatology would not wish that this might be true?

POSTSCRIPT
ROBERT G. CLOUSE

A critical individual may well ask, "Why spend so much time and energy trying to understand biblical teaching on eschatology?" The argument could continue with the critic pointing out that the doctrine of the future has been one of the most divisive elements in recent Christian history. Indeed, if the only problem involved in such teaching were abstract speculation about coming events, one might be tempted to ignore the entire affair. This is not possible, however, because many attitudes that a Christian has about society, the church and its purpose, education and culture, and even current events are conditioned by the sort of eschatology he holds.

Since the most common form of millennialist teaching is that of the premillennialist, the following remarks will be directed especially to that position. An individual who takes a premillennial view will generally be more pessimistic about society than those who accept one of the other eschatologies. As one writer recently stated,

But how can anyone be stable in a world like ours? A dog-eat-dog attitude pervades business affairs. The materialism of this day of plenty puts pressure on all of us. Increased

income has brought increased spending and greater pres-
sures. Riots in our cities and rebellion against authority in
general make people afraid to walk the streets. Parents are
afraid for their children, races fight each other, and nations compete to see who can first destroy the others. In the
Church, apostasy, indifference and deadness seem to be
common. False intellectualism is so rampant that we are
told that the unbelievers are the real believers, and that God
is either dead or so far gone as to be for all practical purposes useless.

We cannot help but wonder where the trend will lead.
Has the Church any message for this confused day? . . . The
answer to these questions is in the Bible, and particularly in
an understanding of God's program for the future.[1]
In his view the only hope for humanity is the Second Coming
of Jesus Christ. This discourages involvement in social action
and fosters a supernatural social ethic which supports the
status quo. Many evangelicals, heavily influenced by premillennialism, do not wish to see social change which would im-
prove the lot of their fellow men. Despite the clear teaching
of the Bible that believers are to love their neighbors and help
them physically and spiritually (Mt. 25; Rom. 12:20), far too
many Christians narrow their mission to an attempt to win
souls for Christ.[2]

Often the church is viewed by those who advocate a premillennial position solely as a promotional organization for the
gospel of Christ. High pressure tactics are used to foster a
pessimistic view of the world and an emphasis is placed upon
"winning the last soul" so that Christ will return. (If theological liberals treat the church as a social club, so fundamental
congregations miss the mark by trying to create a countercul-
tural group that engages in propaganda for the Lord's sake.)
In contrast to both of these attitudes, the Scriptures picture
the church as a healing community which not only is used by

God to make men whole but continues to care for each of its members. This concern reaches out to help every area of human need. Consequently, amillennialists and postmillennialists have a much greater appreciation of the church as the cause or community of God which transcends time and space than do many premillennialists. Postmillennialism especially opens the possibility of true revival coming to God's people, and through them exerting a healing influence on all human institutions.

Premillennialists often take an extremely separatist position with regard to culture. They tend to emphasize Bible schools and seminaries that train for "full-time" Christian service. A solid grounding in the liberal arts and a thorough knowledge of the history of Christian thought are not as popular among these groups as they would be among amillennialists and postmillennialists. There is a great danger in this because if Christians neglect the arts and entertainment media, these avenues of expression are usually taken over by more secular, materialistic influences. Rather than working for some sort of synthesis between Christ and culture, many ardent advocates of the millennium preach a message that consists largely of subcultural denials of the prevailing forms of art and expression.

Another aspect of premillennialism that troubles many Christians is the effort to identify the "signs of the times." Often such occurrences as natural disasters, apostasy in the churches, technological advancements and the rise of authoritarian political leaders are cited as proof that "the end is near" and that the Second Coming of Christ is "at hand" or "imminent." At the present time attention is focused on the Middle East and the fortunes of the nation of Israel as pre-eminent signs. Aside from the fact that seeking for signs can lead down the blind alley of date setting, the tendency to identify God's cause with Zionism and the nation of Israel can lend support to policies which do not make for peace on earth. The United States could well be drawn into war in the Middle East and many evangelicals might be responsible for the attitudes that can lead to that conflict.

However, premillennialism is of great value for it focuses attention on eschatology. This is an area that is easy for Christians to ignore. Yet the gospel of Christ is a message of hope and openness to the future. Premillennialism constantly reminds the believer that no matter how discouraging the situation is today, millennial glory awaits. Perhaps one's social class is declining or his conservative theological viewpoint is on the wane or some great personal tragedy has befallen him, yet he may take heart, for one day assuredly he will rule the world with Christ.

As C. S. Lewis warned, however, an eschatology must never preclude

> sober work for the future within the limits of ordinary morality and prudence. . . . For what comes is judgment: happy are those whom it finds laboring in their vocations, whether they were merely going out to feed the pigs or laying good plans to deliver humanity a hundred years hence from some great evil. The curtain has indeed now fallen. Those pigs will never in fact be fed, the great campaign against white slavery or governmental tyranny will never in fact proceed to victory. No matter; you were at your post when the inspection came.[3]

NOTES

Introduction

[1] Norman Cohn, *The Pursuit of the Millennium* (New York: Oxford University Press 1970).

[2] Calvin branded those who were interested in millennialism with such names as "ignorant" or "malicious." John Calvin, *Institutes of the Christian Religion*, ed. J. T. McNeil, trans. F. L. Battles, II (Philadelphia: Westminster Press, 1960), III, 25, 996. Note also Heinrich Quistorp, *Calvin's Doctrine of the Last Things*, trans. H. Knight (Richmond, Virginia: John Knox Press, 1955).

[3] Robert G. Clouse, "Johann Heinrich Alsted and English Millennialism," *Harvard Theological Review*, LXII (1969), 189-207.

[4] Robert G. Clouse, "The Apocalyptic Interpretation of Thomas Brightman and Joseph Mede," *Journal of the Evangelical Theological Society*, XI (1968), 181-93. For details about Puritan millenarianism note Philip G. Rogers, *The Fifth Monarchy Men* (New York: Oxford University Press, 1966), and Peter Toon, ed., *Puritans, the Millennium and the Future of Israel, Puritan Eschatology 1600-1660* (Cambridge: James Clarke & Co., 1970).

[5] One of the most famous orthodox Christian postmillennialists of the eighteenth century was Jonathan Edwards. A suggestive analysis of his ideas is contained in James Carse, *Jonathan Edwards and the Visibility of God* (New York: Charles Scribner's Sons, 1967).

[6] Ernest R. Sandeen, *The Roots of Fundamentalism, British and American Millenarianism* (Chicago: University of Chicago Press, 1970).

[7] Clarence Bass, *Backgrounds to Dispensationalism* (Grand Rapids, Michigan: William B. Eerdmans, 1960).

[8] For a critical analysis of the Scofield Bible see Loraine Boettner, *The Millennium* (Philadelphia: Presbyterian and Reformed Publishing Co., 1957), pp. 369-73.

[9] Hal Lindsey, *The Late Great Planet Earth* (Grand Rapids, Michigan: Zondervan Publishing House, 1970); *There's a New World Coming* (Santa Ana, California: Vision House, 1973); and *The Terminal Generation* (Old Tappan, New Jersey: Fleming H. Revell, 1976).

Chapter One

[1] Charles Ryrie, *Dispensationalism Today* (Chicago: Moody Press, 1965).

[2] Ibid., p. 45.

[3] Ibid.

[4] John Walvoord, *The Millennial Kingdom* (Findlay, Ohio: Dunham, 1959), p. 71.

[5] Ibid.

[6]Ryrie, p. 46.
[7]Walvoord, p. 312.
[8]See G. E. Ladd, "Apocalyptic, Apocalypse" in *Baker's Dictionary of Theology*, ed. E. F Harrison (Grand Rapids, Michigan: Baker Book House, 1960), pp. 50-54.
[9]This is argued in detail in G. E. Ladd, *A Commentary on the Revelation of John* (Grand Rapids, Michigan: William B. Eerdmans, 1972).
[10]Henry Alford, *The Greek Testament* (Boston: Lee and Shepard, 1872), IV, p. 732.
[11]J. F. Walvoord, Review of *The Presence of the Future*, in *Bibliotheca Sacra* (July 1974), p. 273.
[12]See G. E. Ladd, "The Parable of the Sheep and Goats in Recent Interpretation," *Twenty-fifth Anniversary Volume of the Evangelical Theological Society* (1975).
[13]This exegesis is defended by Oscar Cullmann, "The Kingdom of Christ and the Church in the New Testament," in *The Early Church*, ed. by A. J. B. Higgins (Philadelphia: Westminster, 1956), pp. 111ff.

Chapter Two
[1]John Bright, *The Kingdom of God* (New York: Abingdon Press, 1953), pp. 7, 197.
[2]John F. Walvoord, *The Millennial Kingdom* (Findlay, Ohio: Dunham, 1959), p. 114.
[3]Oswald Allis, *Prophecy and the Church* (Philadelphia: Presbyterian and Reformed Publishing Co., 1945), p. 238.
[4]Floyd Hamilton, *The Basis of Millennial Faith* (Grand Rapids, Michigan: William B. Eerdmans, 1942), p. 38.
[5]Alva J. McClain, *The Greatness of the Kingdom* (Grand Rapids, Michigan: Zondervan Publishing House, 1959), pp. 527-31.
[6]Herman A. Hoyt, *The End Times* (Chicago: Moody Press, 1969), pp. 168-70.
[7]McClain, p. 17.
[8]Conrad Von Orelli, "History of Israel," in *International Standard Bible Encyclopaedia*, 2nd ed., (Chicago: The Howard-Severance Co., 1929), III, 1515.
[9]McClain, p. 383.

Responses
[1]John F. Walvoord, *Matthew: Thy Kingdom Come* (Chicago: Moody Press, 1955), p. 30.

Chapter Three
[1]From Loraine Boettner, *The Millennium* (Philadelphia: Presbyterian and Reformed Publishing Co., 1957), pp. 14-16, 18-22, 30, 35, 38-41, 43-44, 47-48, 50-51, 52-53, 58-59, 82-86, 98-101. The author has revised this essay and supplied it with more recent figures.
[2]J. Marcellus Kik, *An Eschatology of Victory* (Philadelphia: Presbyterian and Reformed Publishing Co., 1971), p. 250.
[3]Albertus Pieters, *Studies in the Revelation of St. John* (Grand Rapids, Michigan: Zondervan Publishing House, 1937), p. 165.
[4]John F. Walvoord, "The Theological Context of Premillennialism," *Bibliotheca Sacra*, 108, No. 431.(1951), pp. 272f.
[5]Jesse F. Silver, *The Lord's Return* (New York: Fleming H. Revell Co., 1914), p. 209.

Chapter Four

[1]Jay E. Adams, *The Time Is at Hand* (Philadelphia: Presbyterian and Reformed Publishing Co., 1970), pp. 7-11.

[2]William Hendriksen, *More Than Conquerors* (Grand Rapids: Baker Book House, 1939). An exposition and defense of this method of interpretation, summarized in nine propositions, can be found on pp. 11-64.

[3]For an expanded exposition of these verses, see Hendriksen, pp. 221-29.

[4]Leon Morris, *The Revelation of St. John* (Grand Rapids, Michigan: William B. Eerdmans, 1969), p. 236.

[5]As a matter of fact, even if *ezēsan* is interpreted to mean a bodily resurrection, the verse still does not describe the earthly millennium commonly held to by premillennialists. For on the basis of the common premillennial interpretation of Revelation 20:4, it is only *raised believers* who are said to reign with Christ; nothing is said in this passage about a reign of Christ over people who have not died but are still living. The millennium of the premillennialists, however, is said to be primarily a reign of Christ over people who are still alive when Christ comes and over their descendants!

[6]John F. Walvoord, *The Millennial Kingdom* (Findlay, Ohio: Dunham, 1959), p. 128.

[7]Ibid., p. 130.

[8]See Martin J. Wyngaarden, *The Future of the Kingdom in Prophecy and Fulfillment* (Grand Rapids, Michigan: Zondervan Publishing House, 1934) for an elaboration and demonstration of the amillennial method of interpreting prophecy. This work is particularly valuable in that it shows how the New Testament spiritualizes many Old Testament concepts: Zion, Jerusalem, the seed of Abraham, Israel, the temple, sacrifices and so on.

[9]This and the following passage (Is. 65:17-25) are quoted from the New Scofield Bible (New York: Oxford University Press, 1967) which gives the King James Version with only a few minor revisions.

[10]Walvoord, p. 298.

[11]Walvoord's comment that the animals mentioned here are creatures of earth and not of heaven does not rule out the possibility that these words may be a prophetic description of conditions on the new earth.

[12]Walvoord, p. 325.

[13]Ibid., pp. 253, 318-19.

[14]Note that in 11:9 Isaiah adds the reason why "they shall not hurt nor destroy": "for the earth shall be full of the knowledge of the Lord, as the waters cover the sea." Surely this condition will be realized only on the new earth in the life to come (see Rev. 21:27; 22:14-15). The last-quoted words cannot be a description of the millennium since during the millennium, according to premillennial teaching, there will still be disobedient nations which must be ruled with a rod of iron!

[15]See Anthony A. Hoekema, *The Christian Looks at Himself* (Grand Rapids, Michigan: William B. Eerdmans, 1975).

[16]Note, for example, how John tells us that the spirit of the Antichrist is already in the world in his day (1 Jn. 4:3).

[17]G. C. Berkouwer, in his recent book, *The Return of Christ* (Grand Rapids, Michigan: William B. Eerdmans, 1972), shows how Scripture requires us to think of the "signs of the times" as having relevance throughout the entire Christian era (pp. 235-59).

[18]Scripture proof for a single general resurrection has been given above in the exposition of Revelation 20:1-6. For additional evidence against a multiple resurrection, see L. Berkhof, *Systematic Theology* (Grand Rapids, Michigan: William B. Eerdmans, 1941), pp. 724-27.

[19]Gerhard Kittel, ed., *Theological Dictionary of the New Testament*, trans. and ed. Geoffrey Bromiley (Grand Rapids, Michigan: William B. Eerdmans, 1964), I, 380-81.

[20]See the excellent chapter on the new earth in Berkouwer, pp. 211-34.

Postscript

[1]Charles C. Ryrie, *The Bible and Tomorrow's News* (Wheaton, Illinois: Scripture Press, 1969), p. 12.

[2]For more about the lack of social concern among premillennialists see Robert G. Clouse, "The Evangelical Christian, Social Concern, and a Theology of Hope," *The Evangelical Quarterly*, XLIV (1972), 68-75. It is necessary to point out that not all premillennial believers abstain from preaching social change. An outstanding example of a leading premillennial theologian who takes a strong stand for social justice is Vernon C. Grounds. See his *Revolution and the Christian Faith* (Philadelphia: J. B. Lippincott, 1971), and for an attempt by Grounds to square his eschatology with his fine social message notice his articles "Premillennialism and Social Pessimism," in *Christian Heritage*, Sept. 1974, pp. 25-27 and Oct. 1974, pp. 28-29. Also one needs to be reminded that those who follow another eschatological belief do not necessarily take a more kindly view of social change.

[3]C. S. Lewis, "The Christian Hope," *Eternity* (March 1954), p. 50.

SELECTED BIBLIOGRAPHY

History of Doctrine
Bass, Clarence B. *Backgrounds to Dispensationalism*. Grand Rapids, Michigan: William B. Eerdmans, 1960.
Bethune-Baker, James F. *An Introduction of the Early History of Christian Doctrine*. London: Methune & Co., 1923.
Case, Shirley Jackson. *The Millennial Hope*. Chicago: University of Chicago Press, 1918.
Cohn, Norman. *The Pursuit of the Millennium*. New York: Oxford University Press, 1970.
Danielou, Jean. *The Development of Christian Doctrine before the Council of Nicaea*. Chicago: Henry Regnery Co., 1964.
Elliott, E. B. *Horae Apocalypticae; or a Commentary on the Apocalypse, Critical and Historical*. 4 vols. London: Seely, Burnside, and Seely, 1847.
Fixler, Michael. *Milton and the Kingdoms of God*. Evanston, Illinois: Northwestern University Press, 1964.
Froom, LeRoy Edwin. *The Prophetic Faith of Our Fathers*. 4 vols. Washington, D.C.: Review and Herald Publishing Association, 1946-1954.
Kelly, John N. D. *Early Christian Doctrines*. New York: Harper & Brothers, 1958.
Klausner, Joseph. *The Messianic Idea in Israel*. New York: Macmillan, 1958.
Kraus, C. Norman. *Dispensationalism in America*. Richmond, Virginia: John Knox Press, 1958.
Morris, Leon. *Apocalyptic*. Grand Rapids, Michigan: William B. Eerdmans, 1972.
Murray, Iain H. *The Puritan Hope*. London: Banner of Truth Trust, 1971.
Peters, George N. H. *The Theocratic Kingdom of Our Lord Jesus, the Christ*. 3 vols. Grand Rapids, Michigan: Baker Book House, 1957.
Sandeen, Ernest R. *The Roots of Fundamentalism*. Chicago: University of Chicago Press, 1970.
Smith, David E. "Millenarian Scholarship in America." *American Quarterly*, XVII, 535-49.
Thrupp, Sylvia, ed. *Millennial Dreams in Action*. New York: Schocken Books, 1969.
Toon, Peter, ed. *Puritans, the Millennium and the Future of Israel*. Cambridge: James Clarke & Co., 1970.
Tuveson, Ernest Lee. *Millennium and Utopia*. Berkeley: University of California Press, 1949.
——————. *Redeemer Nation*. Chicago: University of Chicago Press, 1968.

Historic Premillennialism
Alford, Henry. *The Greek Testament*. New Edition. 4 vols. London: Longmans, Gree & Co., 1894.

Frost, Henry W. *The Second Coming of Christ.* Grand Rapids, Michigan: William B. Eerdmans, 1934.

Guinness, H. Grattan. *The Approaching End of the Age.* London: Hodder and Stoughton, 1880.

Kellogg, S. H. *The Jews, or Predictions and Fulfillment.* New York: A. D. F. Randolph & Co., 1883.

Ladd, George E. *The Blessed Hope.* Grand Rapids, Michigan: William B. Eerdmans, 1956.

——————. *A Commentary on the Revelation of John.* Grand Rapids Michigan: William B. Eerdmans, 1972.

—————— *Crucial Questions About the Kingdom of God.* Grand Rapids, Michigan: William B. Eerdmans, 1952.

——————. *The Gospel of the Kingdom.* Grand Rapids, Michigan: William B Eerdmans, 1959.

—————— *The Presence of the Future.* Grand Rapids, Michigan: William B. Eerdmans, 1974.

Payne, J. Barton. *Encyclopedia of Biblical Prophecy.* New York: Harper and Row 1973.

Reese, Alexander *The Approaching Advent of Christ.* London: Marshall, Morgan & Scott, 1937.

West, Nathaniel. *Studies in Eschatology; The Thousand Years in Both Testaments.* New York: Fleming H. Revell, 1889.

Dispensational Premillennialism

Anderson, Robert. *The Coming Prince.* Grand Rapids, Michigan: Kregel Publications, 1969.

Blackstone, William E. *Jesus Is Coming.* New York: Fleming H. Revell, 1908.

Brookes, James H. *Maranatha.* 10th ed. New York: Fleming H. Revell, 1889.

Chafer, Lewis Sperry. *Dispensationalism.* Dallas: Dallas Seminary Press, 1936.

——————. *Systematic Theology.* Dallas: Dallas Seminary Press, 1947-48. Vol. 4 deals with eschatology.

Darby, John N. *Synopsis of the Books of the Bible.* 2nd ed. 5 vols. New York: Loizeaux Brothers, 1950.

Ehlert, Arnold H. "A Bibliography of Dispensationalism," *Bibliotheca Sacra*, 1944-1946.

Feinberg, Charles L. *Premillennialism or Amillennialism?* 2nd ed. Wheaton, Illinois: Van Kampen Press, 1954.

Gaebelein, Arno C. *The Hope of the Ages.* New York: Publication Office "Our Hope," 1938.

—————— *The Return of the Lord.* New York: Publication Office "Our Hope," 1925.

Gray, James M. *Prophecy and the Lord's Return.* New York: Fleming H. Revell, 1917.

Haldeman, I. M. *The Coming of Christ, Both Premillennial and Imminent* New York: Charles C Cook, 1906.

Hoyt, Herman A. *The End Times.* Chicago: Moody Press, 1969.

Ironside, H. A. *The Lamb of Prophecy.* Grand Rapids: Zondervan, 1940.

Lindsey, Hal. *The Terminal Generation.* Old Tappan, New Jersey: Fleming H. Revell, 1976

————————. *The Late Great Planet Earth.* Grand Rapids, Michigan: Zondervan, 1970.

————————. *There's a New World Coming.* Santa Ana, California: Vision House, 1973.

McClain, Alva J. *The Greatness of the Kingdom.* Grand Rapids, Michigan: Zondervan, 1959.

Pache, Rene. *The Return of Jesus Christ.* Translated by William Sanford La Sor. Chicago: Moody Press, 1955.

Pentecost, J. Dwight. *Prophecy for Today.* Grand Rapids, Michigan: Zondervan, 1961.

————————. *Things To Come.* Findlay, Ohio: Dunham, 1959.

Peters, George N. H. *The Theocratic Kingdom of Our Lord Jesus, the Christ.* 3 vols. Grand Rapids, Michigan: Baker Book House, 1957.

Ryrie, Charles C. *Dispensationalism Today.* Chicago: Moody Press, 1965.

Sauer, Erich. *From Eternity to Eternity.* Grand Rapids, Michigan: William B. Eerdmans, 1954.

Scofield, C. I. *Rightly Dividing the Word of Truth.* New York: Fleming H. Revell, 1907.

————————, ed. *The Scofield Reference Bible.* New York: Oxford University Press, 1909.

————————, ed. *The New Scofield Bible.* New York: Oxford University Press 1967.

Walvoord, John F. *The Millennial Kingdom.* Findlay, Ohio: Dunham, 1959.

————————. *The Rapture Question.* Findlay, Ohio: Dunham, 1957.

Wood, A. Skevington. *Signs of the Times.* Grand Rapids, Michigan: Baker Book House, 1971.

Postmillennialism

Boettner, Loraine. *The Millennium.* Philadelphia: Presbyterian and Reformed Publishing Co., 1957.

Brown, David. *Christ's Second Coming.* 6th ed. Edinburgh: T. & T. Clark, 1867.

Campbell, Roderick. *Israel and the New Covenant.* Philadelphia: Presbyterian and Reformed Publishing Co., 1954.

Hodge, Charles. *Systematic Theology.* New York: Scribner's, 1871.

Kik, J. Marcellus. *An Eschatology of Victory.* Nutley, New Jersey: Presbyterian and Reformed Publishing Co., 1974.

Shedd, W. G. T. *Dogmatic Theology.* New York: Scribner's Sons, 1888.

Snowden, James H. *The Coming of the Lord.* New York: Macmillan, 1919.

Strong, Augustus H. *Systematic Theology.* Philadelphia: Griffith and Roland Press, 1907.

Warfield, B. B. *Biblical Doctrines.* New York: Oxford University Press, 1929.

Amillennialism

Allis, Oswald T. *Prophecy and the Church.* Philadelphia: Presbyterian and Reformed Publishing Co., 1945.

Berkhof, Louis. *Systematic Theology.* Grand Rapids, Michigan: William B. Eerdmans, 1941.

————————. *The Second Coming of Christ.* Grand Rapids, Michigan: William B. Eerdmans, 1953.

Berkouwer, G. C. *The Return of Christ.* Grand Rapids, Michigan: William B. Eerd-mans, 1972.

Cox, William E. *Amillennialism Today.* Philadelphia: Presbyterian and Reformed Publishing Co., 1972.

——————— *An Examination of Dispensationalism.* Philadelphia: Presbyterian and Reformed Publishing Co., 1971.

——————— *Biblical Studies in Final Things.* Philadelphia: Presbyterian and Reformed Publishing Co., 1967.

Graebner, Theodore. *War in the Light of Prophecy.* St. Louis: Concordia Publishing House, 1941.

Grier, William J. *The Momentous Event.* Belfast: Evangelical Bookshop, 1945.

Hamilton, Floyd E. *The Basis of Millennial Faith.* Grand Rapids, Michigan: William B. Eerdmans, 1942.

Hendriksen, William. *More Than Conquerors.* Grand Rapids, Michigan: Baker Book House, 1939.

Hodges, Jesse Wilson. *Christ's Kingdom and Coming.* Grand Rapids, Michigan: William B. Eerdmans, 1957.

Hoekema, Anthony A. *The Bible and the Future.* Grand Rapids, Michigan: William B. Eerdmans, 1979.

Hughes, Archibald. *A New Heaven and a New Earth.* Philadelphia: Presbyterian and Reformed Publishing Co., 1958.

Jones, R. Bradley, *What, Where, and When Is the Millennium?* Grand Rapids, Michigan: Baker Book House, 1975.

Kuyper, Abraham. *Chiliasm, or the Doctrine of Premillennialism.* Grand Rapids, Michigan: Zondervan Publishing House, 1934.

Masselink, William, *Why Thousand Years?* Grand Rapids, Michigan: William B. Eerdmans, 1930.

Mauro, Philip. *The Seventy Weeks and the Great Tribulation.* Swengel, Pennsylvania: Bible Truth Depot, 1944.

Morris, Leon. *The Revelation of St. John.* Grand Rapids, Michigan: William B. Eerdmans, 1969.

Murray, George L. *Millennial Studies.* Grand Rapids, Michigan: Baker Book House, 1948.

Pieters, Albertus. *Studies in the Revelation of St. John.* Grand Rapids, Michigan: Zondervan Publishing House, 1937.

——————— *The Seed of Abraham.* Grand Rapids, Michigan: William B. Eerdmans, 1950.

Travis, Stephen. *The Jesus Hope.* Downers Grove, Illinois: InterVarsity Press, 1976.

Vos, Geerhardus. *The Pauline Eschatology.* Grand Rapids, Michigan: William B. Eerdmans, 1930.

Wilcock, Michael. *I Saw Heaven Opened.* Downers Grove, Illinois: InterVarsity Press, 1975.

Wyngaarden, Martin J. *The Future of the Kingdom.* Grand Rapids, Michigan: Baker Book House, 1955.

CONTRIBUTING AUTHORS

Loraine Boettner was born in northwest Missouri. He is a graduate of Princeton Theological Seminary (Th.B., 1928; Th.M., 1929), where he studied Systematic Theology under the late Dr. C. W. Hodge. Previously he had graduated from Tarkio College, Missouri, and had taken a short course in Agriculture at the University of Missouri. In 1933 he received the honorary degree of Doctor of Divinity, and in 1957 the degree of Doctor of Literature. He taught Bible for eight years in Pikeville College, Kentucky. A resident of Washington, D.C., eleven years, and of Los Angeles three years, his present home is in Rock Port, Missouri. His books include *The Reformed Doctrine of Predestination* (1932), *Studies in Theology* (1947), *Immortality* (1956) and *Roman Catholicism* (1962).

Robert G. Clouse is Professor of History at Indiana State University, Terre Haute, and also is an ordained Brethren minister, having served churches in Iowa and Indiana. He graduated from Bryan College (B.A.), Grace Theological Seminary (B.D.) and the University of Iowa (M.A. and Ph.D.). He is a student of the history of Christian thought. Professor Clouse has coedited *Protest and Politics* (1968) and has contributed chapters to *Puritans, The Millennium and the Future of Israel* (1970), *Christ and the Modern Mind* (1972) and *The Cross and the Flag* (1972).

Anthony A. Hoekema was born in the Netherlands and immigrated to the United States in 1923. He attended Calvin College (A.B.), the University of Michigan (M.A.), Calvin Theological Seminary (Th.B.) and Princeton Theological Seminary (Th.D., 1953). After serving as minister of several Christian Reformed Churches (1944-56) he became Associate Professor of Bible at Calvin College (1956-58). Since 1958 he has been Professor of Systematic Theology at Calvin Theological Seminary. Professor Hoekema spent two sabbatical years in Cambridge, England (1965-66, 1973-74) and has written *The Four Major Cults* (1963), *What about Tongue-Speaking?* (1966), *Holy Spirit Baptism* (1972), *The Christian Looks at Himself* (1975) and *The Bible and the Future* (1979).

Herman A. Hoyt is Chancellor and Professor of Christian Theology at Grace Theological Seminary and Grace College, located at Winona Lake, Indiana. He holds the A.B., B.D., M.Th., and Th.D. degrees, as well as the honorary degree of LL.D. He has written *The End Times* (1969) and a volume on "The Attributes of God" is forthcoming. He is also a contributor to a number of national Christian periodicals and a symposium on the millennium. Dr. Hoyt is presently President of the Board of Directors of Winona Lake Christian Assembly and was associated with Dr. Alva J. McClain, first President of Grace Theological Seminary and Grace College when it was founded in 1937.

George Eldon Ladd, Professor of New Testament exegesis and theology at Fuller Theological Seminary since 1950, was educated at Gordon College and Gordon Divinity School (B.D.) and received the Ph.D. degree from Harvard University. He has also done postdoctoral study at Heidelberg and Basel Universities. Ordained as an American Baptist minister, Dr. Ladd has served several churches of that denomination. He was Professor of Greek at Gordon College (1942-45) and head of the department of New Testament at Gordon Divinity School (1946-50). His writings include *Crucial Questions about the Kingdom of God* (1952), *The Blessed Hope* (1956), *The Gospel of the Kingdom* (1959), *Jesus Christ and History* (1963), *The New Testament and Criticism* (1965), *The Pattern of New Testament Truth* (1968), *Commentary on The Revelation* (1972) and *The Theology of the New Testament* (1974).

Other Four-Views Books

Predestination and Free Will edited by David Basinger and Randall Basinger. Four scholars argue varying views of how divine sovereignty can be reconciled with human freedom.

Women in Ministry, edited by Bonidell Clouse and Robert G. Clouse. Four authors debate what roles in Christian ministry are open to women.